DATE DUE			

Management information systems in higher education: the state of the art

Management information systems in higher education: the state of the art.

Edited by Charles B. Johnson and William G. Katzenmeyer

Duke University Press   Durham, North Carolina   1969

© 1969, Duke University Press
L.C.C. card no. 74-109171
S.B.N. 8223-0233-0

378.1
Se 5m
78759
June / 1972

Printed in the United
States of America

Preface

The Seminar on Management Information Systems: The State of the Art, held at Duke University, June 24-27, 1969, and the publication of the seminar papers are the direct outgrowth of a series of projects sponsored by the Esso Foundation under the foundation's Support for Promoting Utilization of Resources program. The support of Mr. George M. Buckingham, Executive Director of the Esso Foundation, and Dr. Frederick deW. Bolman, Associate Director, is gratefully acknowledged.

As universities have grown in enrollment and budget and as their functions have become more complex, with respect to both internal and external commitments and responsibilities, the management of universities has become an increasingly difficult task. Intelligent decision making requires a great variety of complex information if it is to be carried forward effectively toward the end that the utilization of the human, physical, and financial resources of the university will be optimized. The existence of the electronic computer has changed the context within which management decisions are made. Administrators since Adam have been making judgements based on incomplete data. Surely Adam's original sin could have been avoided if only he had possessed the appropriate data with which to make his decisions. He didn't have that information, however — which somehow explains our dilemma.

In spite of the lesson of Adam, administrators everywhere continue practicing the art of the possible. They choose the best decision alternative on the basis of whatever information is available to them as an input to the decision making process. Other factors being equal, the administrator with the greatest amount of relevant information available is in the best position to make a decision. It is obvious that a physician who fails to heal a patient suffering from a disease for which a cure is known to other physicians. In a similar sense the computer has changed the context in which the decision making process is carried forward. If adequate information is not and cannot be made available, the decision must be made, nonetheless, on such information as is available. If, on the other hand, information that could substantially improve the basis for decision making is or could be available, making a decision in the absense of such data is irresponsible management practice. The existence of the computer and the competence to utilize it in the development of management information are making the creation of management information systems imperative to ethical administrative practice in complex institutions.

Determining that a management information system is needed is a first step. The problems of developing such a system, once this decision is made, are formidable. Many of the early efforts in the development of such systems have failed. Many more have become routine data-processing operations. A few have contributed significantly to the quality of decisions being made in the university. There are a number of factors which determine whether a particular effort will fall into one or another of the above categories. These factors include the basic notions of the institution about the function of management, the skill and creativity of the individuals developing the system, the vision of the administration, the organizational position of the data system within the operational milieu of the university, the resources allocated to the development project, and the systems approach employed.

At present, the administrator who sees the need and the responsibility for the development of an adequate management information system can find little assistance in published form. Only a modicum of information is available that will enable him to utilize the accumulated experience of others in making decisions relative to the building of a successful system at the lowest cost with the highest return on his investment.

Included in this volume is a discussion of certain principles and procedures involved in the development of management information systems as well as specific suggestions drawn out of practical experience. Each of the authors of the chapters in this volume has demonstrated vision, competence, and creativity in the development of management information systems. The insights, hindsights, and foresights derived from these efforts

are offered in this volume, both as an orientation to the field
of management information systems and as a guide to initial
planning of such systems.

For effective planning at the regional and national level,
the data system must provide data for external as well as
internal use. Because the primary function of information
systems is in the area of internal management, the development of overlying systems presents a diverse set of problems.
The papers in Part II provide insights into two creative
efforts to cope with the problems of large-scale interinstitutional information systems.

Finally, modeling or simulation is a promising and exciting
resource in the development of management systems. This volume
provides an introduction to the basic notions in the application of modeling techniques to management problems in higher
education management.

In summary, this volume has three major functions and is
organized into parts by these functions. The primary function
of Part I is to provide basic information about the approaches
to management information systems in the aspects of development, theory, principles, organization, and resource allocation. The function of Part II is to provide basic information about the development of large-scale multi-institutional
information systems, their development to date, and the probable future course such systems will follow. It is hoped
that the material in Part III will interest the reader in the
potential of modeling or simulation techniques as a management tool by providing rudimentary knowledge about the
techniques and illustrations of application to a problem in
higher education.

While none of the chapters in the volume is the final word
on the subject with which it deals, in total these chapters
and the orginal papers on which they draw represent the best
thinking of the men from across the United States who have
been directly involved in the development of some of our most
effective university management information systems. It is
hoped that this volume will be a useful sourcebook for those
considering the development of a management information system,
for those already charged with the development of such a system,

and for students or faculty interested in higher educational administration.

At the conclusion of several of the chapters there are comments from both the editors and the commentators. These comments may raise additional questions and suggest alternative perspectives on the subject of each paper.

The editors acknowledge their debt to the authors as well as the commentators who contributed greatly to the development of the chapters which appear here.

Dr. Charles B. Johnson
Associate Professor,
Department of Education
Dr. William G. Katzenmeyer
Associate Professor,
Department of Education

Duke University
Durham, North Carolina
September 1969

Contributors

Authors

George W. Baughman is Director of Administrative Research at the Ohio State University

Ronald Brady is Assistant Provost at the Ohio State University

John Chaney is Director of Administrative Data Processing at the University of Illinois

Theodore Drews is Chief, Higher Education Surveys Branch, National Center for Educational Statistics in the U.S. Office of Education, Washington, D.C.

Mrs. Sheila Drews is Research Analyst with the Institutional Research and Planning Office at the Catholic University of America

Ben Lawrence is Program Director Designate of the Western Interstate Commission for Higher Education

Ralph Van Dusseldorp is Associate Professor of Education Administration at the University of Iowa

Robert Wallhaus is Assistant Director of Administrative Data Processing at the University of Illinois

Martin Zeigler is Associate Provost at the University of Illinois

Ronald L. Jensen is Associate Professor of Business Administration at Emory University

Martin L. Levin is Assistant Professor of Sociology at Emory University

William Pendleton is at Emory University

Norman P. Uhl is at Emory University

F. William Arcuri is at the University of Rochester

Thomas R. Mason is Director of the Office of Institutional Research at the University of Colorado

Mark Meredith is Acting Administrator at the University of Rochester

Clark R. Cahow is University Registrar of Duke University

Joe McDonald is a graduate student in research at Duke University

Roger Wilkins is a graduate student in research at Duke University

Commentators

Joseph Battle, Director of Operations Analysis and Institutional Research, Shaw University

George Baughman, Director of Administrative Research, Ohio State University

Dennis K. Blossom, Assistant to Controller, University of Missouri

Ronald Brady, Assistant Provost, Ohio State University

John Caffrey, Director, Commission on Administrative Affairs, American Council on Education

Donald E. Cunningham, Dean for Research, Miami University

Clarence Daniel, Vice-President and Business Manager, Rensselaer Polytechnic Institute

Ted Davis, Financial Vice-President for Business, University of Utah

John Hamblen, Director, Computer Sciences Project, Southern Regional Education Board

Peggy Heim, Director, Planning Center, Furman University

Dean Hirt, Director of Administrative Systems, University of Colorado

James Hitt, Director of Systems Development, University of Kansas

Hans Jenny, Vice-President for Budgetary Affairs, The College of Wooster

Dennis Jones, Assistant Vice-President and Business Manager, Rensselaer Polytechnic Institute

Alan C. Kerckhoff, Professor, Sociology Department, Duke University

Robert Koski, Planning Officer, Long Range Planning Office, University of Washington

Thomas Mason, Director, Office of Institutional Research, University of Colorado

James H. McCormick, Associate Professor and Dean of Academic Affairs, Shippensburg State College

Thomas Naylor, Director, Econometric System Simulation Program, Duke University

David Nyman, Systems Analysis, Miami University

Louis Pondy, Associate Professor, Department of Management Sciences, Associate Professor, Community Health Sciences, Duke University

Frank Richardson, Research Economist, Office of Institutional Research, University of Colorado

Joseph Saupe, Director, Institutional Research, University of Missouri

D. Paul Smay, Vice-President for Academic Affairs, Shippensburg State College

Louis Volpp, Dean, Graduate School of Business Administration, Chairman, Department of Management Sciences, Duke University

E. Carl Zimmerman, Director, Computer Services Center, College of Wooster

Contents

Part I. Basic considerations in the development of management information systems.

This section provides an intensive review of the following:

1. The basic philosophic questions of management.
2. The principles that underlie the development of a successful management information system.
3. The form of organization and structure that is most conducive to the development of high-quality systems.
4. Suggestions for appropriate allocation of economic and human resources so that the greatest return in system quality for the dollars invested may be realized.

Each of the authors of the chapters in this section is a successful practitioner in the development of management information systems. The systems they have developed and are developing are recognized for quality, for creativity, and for viability — attributes essential to any effective management information system. That the authors do not agree at each intersection of their respective chapters reflects the application of resourcefulness and creativity of each author to the unique circumstances of his own endeavor. These differences serve to alert us to a reality in the development of new information systems. This reality is that efficient development calls for the effective utilization of principles and practices successfully used by others, together with the creative modification of these principles and practices successfully used by others, together with the creative modification of these principles and practices in response to the unique requirements of a specific institutional context. Each new system, in coping with its unique circumstances, will contribute further to broadening our base of knowledge about the principles and practices that are appropriate to a variety of situations. Each will also help others define courses of action most likely to lead to the development of quality management information systems.

The editors believe that these chapters will be most helpful if read as forming a single though many-sided book, an

1

*attempt to define the basic parameters of successful manage-
ment information systems.*

Chapter one. Towards a theory of university management. *George W. Baughman, in collaboration with Ronald Brady*

Is university management a triplodirty?

Shelley Berman has recently advanced a theory of word implications. He finds that we react to many words and events in a way determined by the society rather than the word content.[1] He was puzzled by the fact that in New Zealand it was quite proper to say in mixed company "I am going to the toilet," whereas in American we studiously avoid the word by saying "little boys' room" or "rest room" or "powder room," or something of the kind. Similarly, in this country, the word "proposition" is quite different than the word "proposal."

He concludes there is a pure sixth sense that, when fully developed, can immediately detect the difference between these word choices and provide an immediate answer to the question, Is it a clean or is it a dirty? For example, "separation" is a clean, "cleavage" is a dirty; "chilly" is a clean, "frigid" is a dirty. In a further refinement of this theory, he advances the notion of a triplodirty — where one clean plus one clean may equal one dirty. Here again, it is the societal reaction to the combination that governs the impact. For example, consider the impact of pairing "athletic" (a clean) and "supporter" (a clean), or perhaps "birth" and "control."

There is much reason to suspect that "university management" is a triplodirty, because it implies something that we apparently would rather not hear in the polite society of higher education. The implication is that someone or some group does exercise the management functions of planning, organizing, and controlling the activities of the university. To avoid this triplodirty, it has become a clean to discuss university management information systems because this phrase avoids any connotation as to who uses the system. In fact, by using the popular "information systems" modifier, it is so clean it almost qualifies as an immaculate.

Armed with a clean, we busy ourselves with the job of
collecting data or building models with the hopes that whoever
does manage will step forward and use them. Unfortunately,
no university management information system can exist without
bona fide users with decision-making responsibility and
authority. Hence, it becomes necessary to make "university
management" a clean: that is, to presume that the management
activities of planning (in the sense of setting objectives,
forecasting, and establishing policy) and organizing (in the
sense of designing ways of performing activities and providing
the resources needed for their performance) and controlling
(in the sense of measuring and evaluating results) are essential and legitimate in the university environment. Further,
we should not tread lightly when talking about university
management, but instead, openly attack the questions of who
does and who should manage the university as well as how they
do manage it and how they should.

Who does manage?

It is clear that there is no common agreement as to what
currently constitutes university management. Certainly
faculty, students, administrators, trustees, alumni, foundations, governmental agencies, industry, religious organizations,
and the general public all have some influence. It is not so
certain which of these groups play the management roles of
directing the activities of the university.

Is it as Mario Savior suggested — "I beg of you to consider:
if this is a firm, and if the Board of Regents are the Board
of Directors...then...the faculty are a bunch of employees
and we're the raw materials?[2] Or is it as Clark Kerr
suggests — "a faculty guild" confronted by "a student class or
lumpen proletariat" with major changes being initiated from
"external imperatives of...trustees, state governments,
foundations, industry and the federal government?[3]

In searching for an answer to the question of university
management (i.e., Who is going to define and attempt to solve
university problems?) we frequently attribute today's problems
to new dimensions of the university. Large bodies of students,

impersonalization of the teaching process, concentrations of federal and foundation grants, inability of the institutions to change, and so on, are not, as we suppose, the problems of the seventies. They are in part a contemporary aspect of university management problems that have existed since the earliest medieval universities.

Knowing that those who cannot remember the past are condemned to repeat it, we should take a close look at our predecessors with the goal of developing a basic philosophy of university management that can withstand the test of time. The intent in presenting this perspective is not to suggest that past patterns yield current solutions. Certainly there are many aspects of today's universities that are quite different from the past. Such things as the size of institutions, the nature of facilities, the degree of specialization, and the relative proportion of persons exposed to the institutions (particularly in the United States) are all significant technical variants from our past. Even if the 30,000 students that the University of Paris claimed in the thirteenth century (for budgetary reasons) had existed, they would have represented a significantly different population in terms of technical needs than the students at that university during the revolution of May 1968. But creative management involves attitudes, goals, and psychic needs as well as technical prescription, and in these nontechnical aspects we are much like our predecessors.

Objectives of the university

The university since its inception has had the primary objective of conserving, augmenting, and promulgating all higher knowledge. As such, the university is a creation of the Middle Ages. The concept of a collection of masters and scholars representing all fields of knowledge would have been as untenable to the Greeks and Romans as the notions of fixed time periods of study, examinations, and degrees. It is difficult to trace the beginnings of this objective, but it seems to have accompanied the influx of new mathematics (arabic numerals), Euclidean geometry, the works of Aristotle,

Ptolemy, and the Greek physicians and the texts of Roman law between 1100 and 1200.

With this objective, the university was able to break the bonds of the monastic and cathedral schools that were still committed to the fifth-century concept of the trivium (grammar, rhetoric, and logic) and the *quadrivium* (geometry, arithmetic, astronomy, and music). It also enabled the university to serve as the portal of entry to all learned professions (law, medicine, theology) and gave it the power to decide what would be taught in preparation for those professions. Even in religious education, Rashdall reports that "although a large segment of students of the arts entered the clergy, the basic arts provided nearly no theological training — except insofar as it taught students to construe their breviary and read in Latin."[4]

A collateral objective of the university has been to provide an academic environment for the secure and pleasurable pursuit of knowledge. We frequently think of the medieval university as a place where faculty and students met and in a solemn, almost monastic manner approached the mysteries of knowledge. The folly of this assumption becomes evident when we see the major impact of the taverns, banquets, loans, housing, clothing, and all the rest, on the life of the masters and scholars. Practical economics (including letter-writing courses designed to solicit funds for food, lodging, books, and travel from parents, friends, and neighbors), special tax exemptions, and rent strikes were all a part of this environment.

In the category of collateral objectives could also be placed the need for establishing and preserving the "mystery and authority" that, in Dostoyevskian terms, must accompany any social "miracle."[5]

In medieval times dress, oaths, customs, title, the exclusive use of Latin, and degrees supported the "mystery" or belief in the social "miracle" called university. The "authority," or affirmation of the validity of the "miracle," could be found in the educated elite who emanated from the universities to assume leadership positions. Further support of the authority appears in a large number of special privileges

accorded the university. Such things as separate judicial
systems, rights to self-determination, and academic freedom
(save in theology) were an integral part of the medieval
university. History is also fraught with numerous and
sometimes extremely violent confrontations of town and
gown, with the university generally emerging as an authori-
tarian victor and with resultant "penance" being paid by the
town.[6]

The modern university attempts to fulfill the same basic
objective of conserving, augmenting, and promulgating all
higher knowledge. In addition, there is considerable evidence
that the collateral objectives of a "proper" environment and
the maintenance of the "mystery and authority" have not been
discarded. Obviously, there are great differences in the
specific means by which we define (by action and policy) and
pursue these objectives. However, these differences tend to
be more in the letter than in the spirit of the university.

The American university, which represents the most radical
break with the past, still attempts to provide an "all knowledge" curriculum and frequently rushes to provide exotic
offerings. The fact that the university in America has been
promoted deliberately as a solution to every man has actually
increased its authority. A land-grant act provided agricultural and mechanical training under the auspices of the
university and led to the ensuing system of providing university degrees in nearly any imaginable field of endeavor (e.g.,
hotel management). The university bachelor's degree, which is
held by so many, has more importance in this country than any
other. It is foolishly required as the entrance price to
many jobs and careers that have no need of it and has become
a disadvantage not to have rather than an advantage to have.

The American university system has perhaps reached a
pinnacle of authority, with over 6,000,000 students — 35
percent of the college-age population. There seems to be a
trend to raise the social mystery of the bachelor's degree to
the master's and Ph.D. level so that every man will in fact
spend time doing graduate study. This trend, however, has
received some serious opposition recently through lack of
legislative enthusiasm for expensive graduate programs and

increased interest, at the post-high-school level, in providing some viable alternative to college.

Attention to student housing, to faculty offices and
emoluments, and to the general campus environment is reflective
of our continuing belief in the need for a creative environment. In other words, we have significantly changed the way
in which the university is used without significantly changing
the overall or collateral objectives.

Functions of the university

The university of today is notably unlike its medieval
counterpart in functional specialization and differentiation.
"Chart I," "The University Environment," suggests the relationships in the functional university environment that we face
in American higher education. The primary objective of conserving, augmenting, and promulgating knowledge is served by
the faculty through the direct functions labeled "Instruction,"
"Research, Creative Work and Development," and "Public Service."
Although we identify these functions and can, in part, classify
specific activities under each one, the functional differentiation is quite incomplete from an organizational standpoint.

Any given faculty member is likely to be performing multiple
functions. There are faculty members who do nothing but research or nothing but teaching or nothing but public service,
but they are exceptions. The reason for distinguishing between
the functions is that they serve quite different populations.
For example, students are primarily served by the instruction
function, although this or that student's academic program may
become entwined with the research or public-service functions.
Government, the public, industry, and the faculty, with their
goals of developing and expanding knowledge, are served by the
research function, which may itself be complementary to the
instruction and public-service functions. Various nonstudent
participants (participants in extracurricular instruction) and
users of specialized university talents are served by the
public-service function, which is itself linked to the instructional and research functions.

The "Academic Environment Support Services" of Chart I include "Student Services" (in support of instruction) and

THE UNIVERSITY ENVIRONMENT

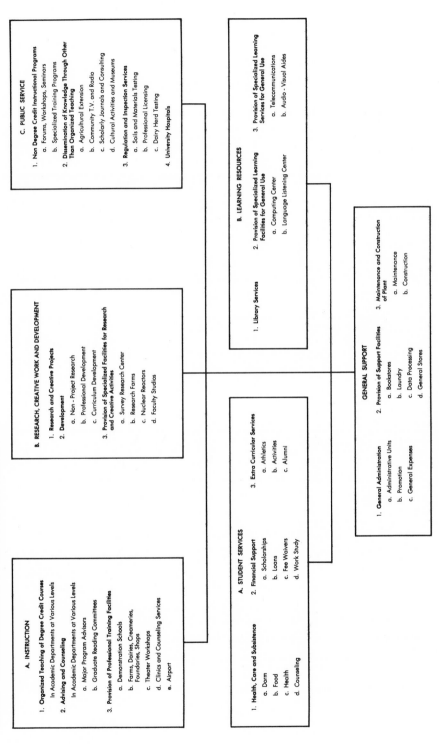

A. INSTRUCTION

1. Organized Teaching of Degree Credit Courses
   In Academic Departments at Various Levels
2. Advising and Counseling
   In Academic Departments at Various Levels
   a. Major Program Advisors
   b. Graduate Reading Committees
3. Provision of Professional Training Facilities
   a. Demonstration Schools
   b. Farms, Dairies, Creameries, Foundaries, Shops
   c. Theater Workshops
   d. Clinics and Counseling Services
   e. Airport

B. RESEARCH, CREATIVE WORK AND DEVELOPMENT

1. **Research and Creative Projects**
2. **Development**
   a. Non - Project Research
   b. Professional Development
   c. Curriculum Development
3. **Provision of Specialized Facilities for Research and Creative Activities**
   a. Survey Research Center
   b. Research Farms
   c. Nuclear Reactors
   d. Faculty Studios

C. PUBLIC SERVICE

1. **Non Degree Credit Instructional Programs**
   a. Forums, Workshops, Seminars
   b. Specialized Training Programs
2. **Dissemination of Knowledge Through Other Than Organized Teaching**
   a. Agricultural Extension
   b. Community T.V. and Radio
   c. Scholarly Journals and Consulting
   d. Cultural Activities and Museums
3. **Regulation and Inspection Services**
   a. Soils and Materials Testing
   b. Professional Licensing
   c. Dairy Herd Testing
4. University Hospitals

A. STUDENT SERVICES

1. Health, Care and Subsistence
   a. Dorm
   b. Food
   c. Health
   d. Counseling
2. Financial Support
   a. Scholarships
   b. Loans
   c. Fee Waivers
   d. Work Study
3. Extra Curricular Services
   a. Athletics
   b. Activities
   c. Alumni

B. LEARNING RESOURCES

1. Library Services
2. Provision of Specialized Learning Facilities for General Use
   a. Computing Center
   b. Language Listening Center
3. Provision of Specialized Learning Services for General Use
   a. Telecommunications
   b. Audio - Visual Aides

GENERAL SUPPORT

1. General Administration
   a. Administrative Units
   b. Promotion
   c. General Expenses
2. Provision of Support Facilities
   a. Bookstores
   b. Laundry
   c. Data Processing
   d. General Stores
3. Maintenance and Construction of Plant
   a. Maintenance
   b. Construction

"Learning Services" (in support of all primary functions). The student-services function is not significantly different in coverage from its medieval counterpart. Problems of housing, feeding, and financial support were just as pressing upon the medieval student and were perhaps sometimes better served in that environment. For example, in 1240 the contract of the students' nation(s?) with the town of Vercilli provided for turning over 500 of the best houses at a guaranteed rent, fixed the prices for food, books, and necessaries that were set by the student organization, and arranged for a rather generous loan fund, in exchange for the students' bringing their university from Padua.[7]

Nearly every university provided students with detailed guides for soliciting funds from parents, relatives, or friends, either through lectures or scholastic manuals. And there are numerous examples in the masters' universities of the beginnings of our own *in loco parentis* statutes of conduct. Only the extracurricular services of student activities, athletics, and alumni activities are true products of the modern university.

The "Learning Services" of Chart I present the newest support function of the academic environment and are still not well differentiated at most of our universities. The library, which did not come into existence until the late Middle Ages, is our most visible learning service. However, we are rapidly arriving at the place where computing centers, audiovisual aids, telecommunications centers, and other clusters of technology will take their places as services that are also recognized to be in support of all three primary functions. Perhaps then we will judge them on their ability to support the primary functions rather than on absolute size.

There is little understanding about the nature of the medieval university with respect to "General Support" services and the functions of providing general administrative services, auxiliary support facilities, and maintenance and construction of plant. Obviously, these functions went on, but apparently the records of them were seldom considered worth preserving. We do know that book production was carried on by the universities in the Middle Ages, but this function fell to the university primarily for the sake of quality control in the correct copying of texts.

The "General Support" function in a modern university is characterized by being much larger and more diverse than in its medieval predecessor. It is far more amenable to comparisons with industry than any other university function, although such comparisons are seldom made. For example, numerous support facilities — bookstores, laundries, general stores, food facilities, binderies, and the like — should be evaluated with traditional business measures (e.g., rate of returns on investment), but seldom are.

In summary, the functions complement the overall objectives of the university, but each poses somewhat different management problems.

Specialization of knowledge

The specialization of knowledge has added to the complexity of the university management environment. As Toynbee has said:

> Since the seventeenth century the amount of potential knowledge has increased far beyond the quantity that can become actual knowledge in a single human mind. Dante did know virtually everything that there was to be known in Western Christendom in the year 1300. Goethe knew the greater part of what there was to be known there in the year 1800. But since 1832, the date of Goethe's death, it has become impossible for even the most powerful intellect and the most industrious temperament to master more than a fraction of what there is to know.[8]

This has led us to the point where specialist speaks to specialist and seldom to anyone else. National Science Foundation specialists may frequently have far more understanding of certain departmental aspirations than the home universities. Countless societies are formed and journals are written for specialty groups.

On the one hand, specialization contributes to a breakdown in communications — all that the faculty is able to discuss in common may be the parking problem — and on the other hand, specialization frequently leads to or is accompanied by integration. In early Egyptian society the development of highly specialized tasks led to a highly integrated society. The

same principle has been applied to the growth of industrial
organizations by various students of management. If we expect
that the specialization of knowledge will be accompanied by an
integration of knowledge, then we should ask how the university,
which reflects this specialization, will participate in the
evolution of integration.

Internal coherence or external integration?

The university has two paths open for its evolution.
Either it will have to achieve internal coherence and present
itself as an entity prepared to deal with the outside world
on an integrated basis, or it will be integrated and assimi-
lated into the outside world through larger extrauniversity
organizations. If we believe in the values of university
autonomy and the academic freedoms that are closely associated
with this autonomy, then the university should organize into
internally coherent patterns and prove to the outside world
that it can and must afford this structure. If we continue
to encourage the patterns of university integration into the
larger worlds of organized national and international coordinating and planning bodies, without developing internal
coherence, then university autonomy becomes a moot question.
It will not be threatened — just bypassed as no longer relevant. Clearly, the question of university management depends
entirely on which path is selected. Faced with the gigantic
forces toward external integration that exist today, the
easier choice is to drift with the tide.

To encourage state coordinating boards to rationalize the
instructional process by providing long- and short-range
instructional goals; to support expansion of federal coordination of research specializations, through the whole range from
the National Institutes of Health and National Science Foundation to the humanities, arts, social sciences, and remaining
professions; and to accede to the demands of students all over
the world for involvement in decision-making by their own fiat
rather than as the institution shall determine — these are
rather simple response mechanisms to today's tides. A far
more difficult task is to face these tides with coherent

institutional goals, objectives, and plans; to accept and
encourage currents that move in consonance with those plans;
and to build dikes to keep out the ones that do not. It is
an enormous undertaking to convince ourselves and others that
academic freedom can be protected only through a reasonably
autonomous university, and that the autonomous university can
innovate and balance its interests with large public interests
and society. But it is this undertaking that serves as the
basis of legitimate university management.

Who should manage?

The objective of the university can now be defined: it is
to provide an institutionally coherent approach to conserving,
augmenting, and promulgating knowledge in consonance with the
goals of larger public interests and society. Management must
plan, organize, and control the activities of the institution
in order to accomplish this objective.

Who can undertake this role in the complex, multifunction,
highly specialized university? The answer is that no one can
and everyone must. In other words, a balanced pluralistic
polity must develop policies, translate them into plans, secure and allocate resources, and control and evaluate performance. Further, these plans and actions must be translated
into a coherent integrated structure for continuous action
with and reaction to the extrauniversity environments. It
must be made clear to the outside world that the university
is in charge and aware of its role and destiny. It must also
be made clear that the university is more capable of defining
its proper total role and destiny than any outside group that
it serves.

There are many ways in which this pluralistic polity with
institutional coherence can be developed. Thus one must take
care not to fall into the trap of setting forth a management
model that should be used, while at the same time defending
the right and value of institutional autonomy. However, at
the very least, a balance should obtain between faculty, students, and administrators. The interfaces that are developed
with the outside world should also be cognizant of and advance

the overall coherent objectives and plans of the university.

Again, history can be of some value in ascertaining past areas of interest and competence on the part of faculty, students, and administrators. In this way it can provide suggestions for the development of management structure.

The role of students. Students have historically been and are today most concerned with the instructional and the student-services functions of the university. The most dramatic evidence of this concern, historically, can be found in the student universities of Italy. Student organizations in Bologna emerged from the scholar-master community and moved rapidly to control, first the services function and then the instructional process (not content). In 1220 students formed a collective and moved against the townspeople, demanding the right for their organization to fix the price of rooms, necessaries, and books. Their overwhelming success with the powerful tool of economic boycott led them next to their second problem...the professors. By threatening to withhold fees, the students were able to bind the professors to some very severe restrictions. Haskins reports:

> Here the threat was a collective boycott and as the masters lived wholly from the fees of their pupils, this threat was equally effective. Professors were put under bond to live up to a minute set of regulations which guaranteed their students the worth of the money paid by each. We read in the earliest statutes that a professor might not be absent without leave, even a single day, and if he desired to leave town, he had to make a deposit to ensure his return. If he failed to secure an audience of five for a regular lecture, he was fined as if absent...a poor lecture indeed which could not secure five hearers! He must begin with the bell and quit within one minute after the next bell. He was not allowed to skip a chapter in his commentary, or postpone a difficulty to the end of the hour, and he was obliged to cover the ground systematically, so much in each specific term of the year.[9]

History is incomplete as to how the student organizations actually functioned in Italy. In general, there were from two to four student nations, based on country of origin (i.e., Italian, French, Provençal, German), each with an elected rector. It is clear that the students were responsible for

the establishment of the University of Padua with a movement
from Bologna.

The Italian universities are credited with having paid more
attention to the instructional process and the evaluation of
instruction than any of their medieval counterparts.

In France, the colleges at the University of Paris were
originally, as elsewhere, merely endowed, student-controlled
residence halls (*hospices*) to provide board and lodging for
scholars who could not afford it. In the course of time, they
became the normal centers of student life and teaching and
were absorbed into the masters' university. There was a college
at Paris as early as 1180, and there were sixty-eight by 1500.

The interest of today's students in more and more relevant
instruction, more reasonable rents, less university control
of their private lives, etc., is certainly well founded in
history. However, in the American university, which followed
the Oxford model, the student has never been a significant
participant in management. Although he has been expected to
plan, organize, and control his way through the labyrinth of
requirements, courses, counselors, dormitories, etc., he has
had little to do with the planning, organizing, and controlling
of this labyrinth. The vestiges of student governance appear
in the form of student assemblies and councils, in occasional
representation on university committees (i.e., "let's have
some student opinion before we do what we are going to do
anyway"), and in various student courts and self-regulatory
associations.

For the most part, the American student has had greatest
involvement with organized social activities. Despite the
lack of real structural integration into key decision points
of the university, students have been able to make some
significant and responsible changes through the structure.
In loco parentis restrictions, speakers' rules, compulsory
R.O.T.C., and discriminatory practices have frequently been
eliminated or substantially reduced through organized student
groups. Likewise, students have recently received increased
representation on various faculty and university committees,
a goal of the National Student Association since the 1950's.

Thus, we see the possibility of the ad hoc development of increased student participation in the decision structure.

A number of students are not willing to wait for evolution. One frequent goal of the Students for a Democratic Society is equal representation among students, faculty, and administrators on all policy-making boards. Such representation is generally found in South America (with the exception of the governing Board, which is frequently all faculty) and has been a major demand of French and German students. The major objection to student representation is the transient status of students. However, most of the accomplishments of students cited above took five to ten years of effort — an indication that while student leaders may change each year, there is a certain consistency in the goals of them all.

A few student leaders have committed themselves to the notion that only a complete structural overhaul can solve the problems of the university (or of society, for that matter). The fact that the nucleus of the group is small, their legitimacy as representatives is questionable, and their tactics odious and destructive (much in the form and manner of the Boston Tea Party), the university will either have to incorporate them into the coherent institutional structure or find ways to reject them as outsiders.

Given the intelligence, dedication, and maturity of many of the students who are interested in change, the incorporation of students into the management structure is both desirable and essential. This is in accord with the general observation of the Cox Commission.

> The student body is a mature and essential part of the community of scholars. This principle has more validity today than ever before in history....The process of drawing students into more vital participation in the governance of the university is infinitely complex. It cannot be resolved by either abstractions or tables of organization. It does not mean that issues must be settled by referenda. *We are convinced, however, that ways must be found, beginning now, by which students can meaningfully influence the education afforded them and other aspects of the university activities.*[10]

Student participation in decision making is not without its disadvantages to the students. In many cases, student leaders who have fought for the right to be heard and to

participate find that the actual work of participation is
arduous and that the process is slow. Frequently, they are
accused of coopting to the establishment, etc., and when given
new facts and understandings find themselves consciously
supporting actions that previously they would have denounced.
In the long run, student participation in decision making may
require more sacrifices on the part of students than on the
part of the institution.

The role of the faculty. The concept of the faculty guild
has been and is the most pervasive notion in university history. In Bologna the faculty guild was a clear counterforce
to the student organization. Membership in the guild of
teachers was determined by examination and led to the award-
ing of a license to teach (*licentia docendi*). Naturally, the
requirements for the degree as well as the examinations themselves were completely under faculty control. Quite as
naturally, the license eventually became the goal of all
students, whether they wanted to teach or not. Parents,
church, and government came to expect the degree as evidence
of successful completion of studies.

In Paris, the model for masters' universities, the professors were organized into four faculties: arts, canon law,
medicine, and theology. The largest, of course, was the
faculty of the arts, and it was subdivided into four nations -
the French, Norman, Picard, and English (including German).
As with the student universities, rectors were elected to serve
for very short terms (three months to one year). The primary
faculty responsibility and interest was in teaching, writing,
examining, and selection of new faculty.

The faculty guilds exhibited high mobility, generally based
on very practical considerations. For example, Rashdall offers
considerable evidence that Oxford was founded, or at least
raised to the stature of a *studium generale* (multidiscipline
university), by an exodus of masters and scholars from Paris
in about 1167. He relates this exodus to the quarrel between
Becket and Henry II and a specific ordinance prohibiting clerks
from crossing from England to the continent without leave of the
king. This same ordinance summoned all clerks who possessed

"revenues" in England, to return within three months "as they loved their revenues."[11]

In many ways, the guild concept is appropriate to describing faculty today. The guild was isolationist toward society, devoted to producer as against consumer sovereignty, committed to guild rules more than quick adaptation to popular demand, eglitarian, full of senatorial courtesy, and selective of its own members.[12] Admittedly, today's faculty member has a far more cosmopolitan view towards the outside world and is quite absorbed in changing it through consulting and applied research. Also, there is far more mobility of faculty into and out of government and industry positions.

The specialization of knowledge, which has caused considerable extrauniversity integration and tended to break down internal cross-communications, has been in great measure countered by the recognition of broad disciplinary interrelationships. Although formal faculty councils seem to communicate best on issues like voting rights for selecting members, the informal faculty world is buzzing with artists talking to mathematicians and information scientists about computer art, doctors talking to sociologists and social workers about urban and social medicine, and so on. Murmurings are also heard about faculty reinvolvement in undergraduate counseling, a function that was delegated to college offices not so long ago. Despite this possibility for improved coherence and change, it must be remembered that faculty are both the champions of and bastions against change.

The two faculty paradoxes are (1) that the faculty represent a radical group by membership and a most conservative one by conduct, and (2) that faculty picture themselves as autonomous, when in fact they have historically always responded to the desires and demands of outside groups. No group has fostered more changes in society and so tenaciously refused to change itself. As Frederick Rudolph concluded, in his study of American Universities,

> resistance to fundamental reform was ingrained in the American college and university tradition, as over three hundred years of history demonstrated....Except on rare occasions, the historic policy of the American college and university was: drift, reluctant accommodation, belated recognition

that while no one was looking, change had in fact taken place.[13]

The internal view of autonomy is heavily based on the mobility and relative independence of the faculty. Yet this same faculty appears to have a high tolerance or adaptability when it comes to external enticements or imperatives. For these reasons change generally comes by adding new things on to the existing structure and only slowly, reluctantly changing the existing structure.

Frequently, faculty members or department chairmen, acting as entrepreneurs, will form an outside alliance with a federal agency or foundation in order to obtain sufficient leverage (through funding) to promote internal change. As Clark Kerr has said,

> When change does come, it may be by the slow process of persuasion, or by subversion as through the inside-outside alliance, or by evasion as in the new enterprise, or by external decision. The academic community, regardless of particular process involved, is more changed than changing; change is more unplanned than planned.[14]

The ideal faculty university is basically a protective one where stability, security, and a sense of equity prevail. Here the inventive individual faculty member can thrive:

> Galileo within the conservative institution of Padua in his day, Erasmus at Oxford and Freiburg, and Newton at Cambridge helped start the enormous metamorphosis from which the modern world emerged. But their institutions, as institutions, were stolidly changeless.[15]

In today's university the resource requirements for supporting the work of the inventive individual faculty member are likely to be enormous. Clearly we have reached a point where individual and departmental entrepreneurship is no longer sufficient to provide these resources. With a proper university management environment for providing these resources, faculty members can remain (or return) to being "oriented toward the problems of disciplines and programs rather than structural and functional problems of the institutions employing them."[16] However, this orientation to disciplines and programs does not mean abrogation of faculty participation in the structural and functional problems. Rather, it means that faculty must constantly work towards making the structural and functional

organization cognizant of and sensitive to the real problems
of disciplines and programs. In the short run this will involve more faculty concern with and awareness of the day-to-
day problems of the institution than they currently have. In
the long run, if their efforts are successful, there will be
a more relevant structural and functional organization to
serve the advancement of their real concerns.

The role of administrators. University administration has
been historically a derived stewardship function. Although
temporal leadership was provided by the elected rectors,
their terms were purposely kept short in both the student
and masters' universities. However, with the medieval pen-
chant for law, rules, and contracts, it was only natural that
clerks would be hired to perform the day-to-day duties of en-
forcing the rules and observing performance on the contracts.
Consider the matter of levying fines in Leipzig in 1438 for a
student throwing or attempting to throw a stone at the master:

   1. Ten new groschen fine for the offense of lifting a
   stone or other missile with a view of throwing it at a
   master, but not actually throwing it.
   2. Eight florins for throwing and missing.
   3. A higher penalty is to be charged for throwing and
   hitting the master, depending on the amount of wounding.[17]

The clerk's job here was to act as a steward for the faculty,
both by administering the rules that the faculty developed and
by collecting and distributing the fines in accordance with
their wishes.

This stewardship function first emerged in connection with
administering student loan funds and was frequently handled by
a monastery or abbey. As universities began to have various
salaried faculty, levy fines, and collect fees for distribution, a minor official called treasurer, receptor, or steward
emerged. When student records, security, and the hiring of
professional assistants became a problem, we encounter the
position of beadle. Initially, both these minor officials
were elected, but eventually they became permanent positions.
Clearly there was no intention that these functionaries would
participate in the management of the enterprise. However, as
the stewards became more responsible for "interpreting" rules

(e.g., what higher penalty will be charged when student X actually hits professor Y), arbitrating feuds between faculty members, and making "equitable" resource allocation decisions (e.g., who gets student loans), they began to look like managers. As the administrative function evolved, the various stewards were used as a buffer against the outside world for interpreting faculty and student needs and securing resources to meet these needs. However, administrators were managers in only a very limited sense. There was little involvement in the planning or organization functions, considerable involvement in the routine control processes. Even budgeting offered little opportunity for anything other than routine planning, because the ground rules were equity, not conscious selection of alternatives.

In general, the functional specialization of stewards from medieval times has prevented university administrators from exercising much management authority. This is evident in financial administration, where considerable attention is directed to controlling expenditures in accordance with fund restrictions; in student administration, where meticulous records of incremental accumulations of courses, points, and credit hours are kept; and in research administration, where the focus is on controlling projects in accordance with grant restrictions. No one, however, is charged with putting these records together, nor are the records designed so that they can be put together. What appears on the surface to be a lack of logical cross-communications channels is nothing more than a highly polished mirror of our old friends the beadle and receptor.

The role of boards of trustees. As John Caffrey has stated, the American experience has been significantly different from the European in that we have not only permitted universities, we have actively created them. We have encouraged private, church-affiliated, municipal, and state universities with vigor. At the same time we have resisted the development of federal universities. For these reasons, the trustee plays a significant role in higher education in the United States.

Our legal notion of the rights of private corporations is
based on the Supreme Court decision in *Dartmouth College* v.
Woodward (1819) and not on a business enterprise. Here the
original charter of King George III to Dartmouth, as a private
eleemosynary institution, was held to be a contract between
the donors and the trustees. The state of New Hampshire was
not permitted to break this contract by changing the charter
and the composition of the trustees to make Dartmouth a state
university. This decision, which is commonly accepted as
contributing to rapid corporate growth in the United States,
also firmly established the rights of trustees as representatives of benefactors of higher education.

Today our universities are faced with a variety of con-
trolling-board situations ranging from self-perpetuating
private boards of control to statewide boards of regents.
In general, these boards serve as a link between the institution and the sponsoring agents, be they private donors, the
church, or the public. Typically, the members of these boards
have little to do with the day-to-day operations of their
institutions. Boards are not composed of faculty, students,
and administrators as in some South American universities.
In fact, they do not typically have any representation from
these populations. Nor are they constituted as a managing
directorate, like many business corporations. There is no
expectation that an administrator will ascend to a board
position or that a board seat will accompany a promotion to
vice-president. For the most part, selection is based on
success in noneducational areas of endeavors (business,
politics, professional life).

A recent survey by Rodney Hartnett of some 5,200 trustees
of 536 institutions revealed that trustees are predominantly
"male (86 percent), at least 50 years old (73 percent), white
(96 percent), well educated (83 percent have at least a
bachelors degree), financially well-off (55 percent have an
income of at least $30,000), protestant (75 percent),
Republican (58 percent), politically moderate (61 percent) or
conservative (21 percent), and more likely to be a business
executive (35 percent) than anything else."[18] Hartnett

stresses that this profile differs markedly from one type of institution to another and by general region.

He found that trustee attitudes about governance also differ considerably by institution. However, some of the general findings are most relevant to the university management question:

1. While a great majority favor the right of free expression for faculty (66 percent), they are reluctant to extend this to campus speakers (69 percent said all campus speakers should be screened) or to eschew faculty loyalty oaths (53 percent favored the loyalty oath).

2. Most trustees would grant a major decision making role to faculty members only on matters of adding or deleting courses and degree programs and on those concerning admissions criteria. Student participation was acknowledged (37 percent favored student participation) in issues related to student cheating and student housing rules, but not at all on issues of academic matters.

3. Despite their general reluctance to grant authority to teachers and students, the trustees themselves were seen as shying away from direct decision making except in selecting the president, in financial affairs, in questions of the physical plant, and in "external questions." On other matters, most of them would rather defer to administrators or at least bring them into the process.

4. The larger the proportion of business executives on the governing board, the smaller the proportion who believe that "running a college is like running a business."

5. In general, the trustees of private universities were more favorable to faculty and student participation in decision making and to a broad interpretation of academic freedom than were the trustees of public institutions. Trustees of private universities generally indicated that their first responsibility was to the institution, whereas trustees of public universities generally indicated that their prime responsibility was to their constituency.

6. In general, board members maintain only a peripheral contact with the institution, and it appeared that "the institu-

tions are not doing enough in the way of keeping their trustees abreast of current thinking."[19]

Because of the diversity of board relationships, the fact that they commonly represent an outside viewpoint (particularly for public universities), and the likely peripheral nature of their contacts, it seems wise to focus on university management from a standpoint of faculty, students, and administrators. This focus is not meant to exclude boards from the management process, but rather to develop a "first line" management concept. That is, a coherent decision structure must exist between faculty, students, and administrators, and this structure must be able to react to and with trustees or other boards of control. The specific degree of involvement of a specific board in the management process is institutionally determined. However, the concept of and need for a university management consisting of faculty, students, and administrators is applicable to any institution regardless of its size, mission, or control.

Providing a decision structure

Clearly the participants have mutual interests in serving the university and in improving it. Likewise, each has competencies that can contribute to the development of a coherent institution which can at the same time remain autonomous (in the sense of self-managed), be innovative, and balance its work with the needs of the outside world. On the other hand, these interests and competencies are in many cases competitive within the structure; for example, students and faculty have vastly different opinions about the instructional process, academic programs compete with each other for the same resources, learning services are more interested in bigger and better libraries and computing centers than they are in faculty salary increases, and so on. For these reasons, a tripartite management of faculty, students, and administrators cannot be a troika, because there is no assurance that it is even possible or desirable to get the parties headed in the same direction. Thus, what we are faced with is the fact that the problem of university management is primarily a political problem and only very secondarily an economic or social one. Wildavsky gives us some direction as to the primary require- ments of a management system based on political rationality:

> Political rationality is the fundamental kind of reason, because it deals with the preservation and improvement of decision structures, and decision structures are the source of all decisions. Unless a decision structure exists, no reasoning and no decisions are possible.[20]

Our first task should be to develop a clear decision structure within the university. Regardless of what decisions are taken or the basis for these decisions, each of the parties should be aware of the decision structure.

Further, the decision structure should be tied closely to the operational structure so that decisions can be made in the context of operational feasibility. In the university, operating as a coherent institution and taking advantage of the interests and capabilities of all parties, the decision structure should be decentralized in the development of goals, objectives, and plans. However, even at this decentralized level it is imperative to consider the political balance and operational aspects of decisions. For example, if a new degree program is envisioned by a departmental faculty, that program should first be considered in context of the departmental goals and with respect to other departmental programs and goals within the college. Further, the implications of the program for other groups, such as student services and learning ser- vices, should be evaluated within the context of the overall goals and capabilities of these groups.

Finally, the decisions should be formulated in a way that they can be carried out within the operating structure, or if a modification to the operating structure is required then this should be incorporated into the plans.

In short, integrated planning should start at the lowest level and work up through a series of evaluation stages seeking political affirmation and operational feasibility at each state. It is imperative that both the method and channels for decision making be clear.

It should be recognized that the decisions taken in this structure will represent compromise, which is always an irra-

tional procedure. The best available proposal will not be
accepted because it is the best. It will be deferred, objected
to, and discussed until major opposition disappears. However,
within the university community the only successful decisions
are ones that can stand the test of compromise.

Supporting university management

The requirements for this kind of management environment are
severe but feasible. The fantastic coordination and communication structures needed to provide for participation among the
various parties and the inordinate demands for relevant and
timely information and analytical support for the evaluation
of decisions at each stage would, at first glance, seem to
defeat the whole proposal. However, with today's interest on
the part of the participants and with the vastly expanded
communications and information=processsing capabilities that
we have, the proposed structure is feasible. It will require
considerable efforts on the part of the president, administrators, faculty, and students. Further, it will require that a
new force be applied to the university to support integrated,
decentralized planning, organizing, and control. This force
will include providing the analytical, informational, planning,
and logistical support to the university and providing the
vehicles for translating the internal goals and objectives of
the institution into the requirements of the outside world
and vice versa. The exciting challenge is that it both can
and must be done.

[Comment by the editors. *The author of this paper may
overestimate the positive effect of interdisciplinary or cross-
disciplinary relations. The development of internal coherence
will probably require more than communication between groups
of scholars in various disciplines as they exchange ideas.
The development of internal coherence depends on the investment of the faculty (as well as of students, administrators,
and controlling boards) in the institution. "Investment"
means that the faculty member must be committed not only to
his discipline but also to the institution. However, the*

rewards which the faculty member may derive from his invest-
ment of self in the institution have been reduced by the
greatly increased size of many universities, the increasingly
specialized character of knowledge (even within a discipline),
and the competing nature of outside funding sources. This
makes the development of internal coherence more difficult and
suggests that the less preferred alternative — external
integration — may be attained more easily. Certainly, many
institutions seem to be moving headlong toward external inte-
gration and give little attention to the problems of internal
coherence.

The image of a university dedicated to integration with
the outside world is unattractive to the editors, but the
establishment and maintenance of internal coherence is prob-
lematic. Not only must the reward structure of the institution
be constituted so as to encourage the investment of the in-
dividual in the institution; it must also be recognized that
internal coherence, once developed, cannot be maintained as
a static entity. Perhaps it should be viewed as a rolling
consensus among students, faculty, administration, and regents;
each must be committed to the maintenance of the institution
as an autonomous entity which can serve the community most
effectively only when it is free from the obligations of ex-
ternal integration.

Internal coherence is not developed to the exclusion of
external integration. Many forces within the autonomous
university assure its continuing responsiveness to the needs
of the larger society. Nevertheless, the primary role defini-
tion of the university must emanate from the faculty, students,
and regents rather than from the imposition of external pres-
sures.]

Notes

1. Shelley Berman, *Cleans and Dirtys*, Los Angeles, Price-
   Stern-Sloan, 1966.
2. Mario Savio, address to Free Speech Movement sit-in,
   University of California at Berkeley, Dec. 2, 1964.
3. Clark Kerr, *The Uses of the University*, Cambridge, Mass.,
   Harvard University Press, 1963.

4. Hastings Rashdall, *The Universities of Europe in the Middle Ages*, vol. 3, pp. 449-50.

5. Fyodor Dostoyevsky, *The Brothers Karamazov*, New York, Random House, 1950, pp. 292-314.

6. Rashdall, vol. 3, p. 101. Perhaps the most striking was the nearly 500 years of penance extracted by the University of Oxford from the town in connection with a raid of the townspeople on the university following a tavern fight on St. Scholastica's Day in 1354. As a part of the penance "on every anniversary of St. Scholastica's Day, the mayor, bailiffs, and sixty burghers were to appear in St. Mary's Church at the Celebration of the Mass, with deacon and subdeacon (at their own expense) for the souls of the slaughtered scholars, and at the offertory, each one of them was to offer one penny at the high alter." This continued until the university "graciously" agreed to forgo its rights after a most humble petition in 1825!

7. Rashdall, vol. 2, app. 1.

8. Arnold Toynbee, Preface to *Campus 1980*, ed. Alvin C. Eurlich, New York, Delacorte Press, 1968, p. xxii.

9. Charles H. Haskins, *The Rise of Universities*, New York, Peter Smith, 1940, p. 15.

10. Cox Commission Report, *Crisis at Columbia*, New York, Vintage Books, 1968, p. 197.

11. Rashdall, vol. 3, pp. 11-32; app. I, pp. 465-76.

12. Kerr, in *Campus 1980*, p. 301.

13. Frederick Rudolph, *The American College and University: A History*, New York, Knopf, 1962, p. 491.

14. Kerr, in *Campus 1980*, p. 305.

15. Kerr, ibid., p. 300.

16. Logan Wilson, ed., *Emerging Patterns in American Higher Education*, "Myths and Realities of Institutional Independence," American Council on Higher Education, Washington, D.C., 1965.

17. Rashdall, vol. 3, p. 363.

18. Rodney T. Hartnett, "Study of the Educational Testing Service at Princeton, N.J.," *Chronicle of Higher Education*, vol. 3, no. 9 (Jan. 13, 1969), p. 1.

19. Hartnett, p. 8.

20. Aaron Wildavsky, "The Political Economy of Efficiency: Cost Benefit Analysis, Systems Analysis, and Program Budgeting," *Public Administration Review*, Dec. 1966, p. 307.

Chapter two. Some principles for the development of management in formation systems.

Ralph Van Dusseldorp

Recently the president of a large university said:

> We were one of the first universities in the country to
> install a computer. We presently have some of the most
> sophisticated computing equipment available. We spend
> over $2,000,000 per year for our computer operations.
> The faculty seems pleased with the computer time and
> equipment available to them for research. We seem to be
> doing a good job of processing student record, payroll,
> etc. by computer. However, I cannot see that the computer
> is helping my administrative staff and myself in planning
> and decision making. When we first installed a computer,
> I understood that one of the benefits would be that the
> administration would be furnished better information for
> planning and decision making. This has simply not come
> about. I cannot see that the administration of this
> university is receiving any benefit from our computer
> operations but still have the feeling that we can and
> should.

This is a very frequent complaint of college administrators
today. Many colleges either have their own computer systems
or have computer time available to them. The computers are
being used extensively and well for faculty and student research. To a somewhat lesser degree they are being used for
processing college records. Little use is being made for
supplying the administration with the information needed for
planning and decision making.

The college administration knows where it is. It knows it
is spending a large amount of money for computer services and
that, although the use of the computer for research and record
processing is quite satisfactory, the furnishing of administrative data is not.

The administration also knows what it wants. It wants to
continue to provide computer facilities for research and to
improve and expand computer processing of university data, but
it also wants better information from the computer facility
for administrative purposes. The administration has a feeling
that this can be got — a feeling that the computer can be used
to provide better administrative information.

The problem is how to go about getting it — how to cause the necessary things to happen so that the administration will get the desired benefits. As has been demonstrated at many institutions, the administration will get little usable management information incidentally as a by-product of computer processing of institutional data. If the administration is to get usable management information, the system must be planned and procedures specifically developed to provide the information.

This is not meant to indicate that a computer is a prerequisite for a college management information system. However, since computers are becoming increasingly available in colleges and since computers can add significantly to management information, parts of this paper are concerned with the development of management information systems in which the computer is a tool for providing some management information.

Information needed for a college to function can be divided into three levels — (1) information for management decisions and planning, (2) information for control, and (3) information for operations.

The lowest level, information for operations, consists of the information needed for clerical functions — payroll, student records, financial transactions, and the like.

The middle level, information for control, involves information needed to implement administrative decisions and policies. For example, a budget for supplies is established for each department on the campus. The administration decides that no department shall be permitted to exceed its supplies budget. Information concerning each department's expenditures for supplies is maintained on a current basis, and controls are established and operate in such a way that orders for supplies in excess of the budgeted amount are automatically rejected. As another example, the administration establishes student performance minimums for promotion from one class to the next. Information concerning the pertinent performance factors of all students is maintained. This information system and the minimum requirements are consulted in promoting students from one class to the next or retaining them in their current class. Thus the information is used to control student promotion.

The highest level, management decisions and planning, involves the use of information in formulating management deci-

sions as well as developing policies and plans. Again, an
example. The president of a state college learns that the
legislature has appropriated the same amount for operation of
the college next year as was appropriated for the current year.
He also knows that income from federal funds will be reduced
next year. In order to obtain enough income to maintain present quality of faculty and programs, he is considering raising
tuition. He needs information on which to base the decision
whether or not to raise tuition, and if the decision is to
raise tuition, how much to raise it. He needs to know how, at
various tuition levels, student enrollment and income from
tuition will be affected. As another illustration the faculty
adviser committee of a college has recommended that the standard
teaching load for faculty members be reduced from 12 hours per
week to 10. The administration knows that if this is done, it
will result in added cost to the university, larger class sizes,
or both. Information is needed concerning the affect on cost,
class size, space utilization, and various combinations of
these factors if the faculty teaching time is reduced as requested. A similar need for information involves the college
president whose students have demanded that classes be taught
only by full-time faculty members, not by graduate assistants.
This president needs information on resultant increases in cost,
class size, and faculty load and their effect on the college
program so he can decide whether to yield to the students' demand. If he decides to yield, he needs to know how to fill the
teaching void left by the graduate assistants.

To date, most of the effort to improve information systems
with the aid of the computer has been directed toward applications at the operations level. Applications to payroll and
student records are relatively easy to develop and are quite
common in colleges today. They result in increased efficiency
of clerical operations, but in and of themselves do little to
improve the administration of the college or provide better
information for decision making and planning. Some progress
has been made in developing improved information systems for
the control functions. Comparatively little effort has been
expended or progress made toward the development of improved
information for management decisions and planning — hence the
frustration of the college administrators mentioned earlier.

Filling the void calls for efforts to develop management information systems. A management information system may be defined as an organized method of providing management with information needed for decisions, when it is needed and in a form which aids understanding and stimulates action. The emphasis is not on information involved in clerical operations, but rather on information needed by management for decision making. Note also that the system is an organized method of providing management information. It does not aim primarily at providing for clerical operations, with management information as an incidental and haphazard by-product.

Let us now examine what has been learned from past experience about the development of information systems in colleges as well as in businesses and industry and see what needs to be done if management information systems are to be successful in colleges.

Concentrated effort is required

If we have learned anything from experience in developing information systems, it is that management information systems do not just happen. They do not automatically result from the development of information systems for operations and control. To say this is not to say that systems for operations and control are unimportant and are unmeaningful applications of information technology, merely that management information systems need concentrated effort for themselves. They do not automatically grow from other information systems. Again, in the past most of our efforts have been directed toward the development of systems for operations and control, not management systems, and we have ended up with just what we aimed at — systems for operations and control, not management systems.

Management must be involved in development

It is not possible to develop a management information system unless management is willing to devote its own time to the effort. Management information systems cannot be developed by systems and information technologists working by themselves or working with personnel at the operations level. The development requires a joint effort of management personnel and information specialists. Only management itself knows what decisions it must make and what information it needs for decision making. In too many cases in the past, management has not been willing or has not seen the need to devote its own time and effort to the development of a management information system. As a result, the new computerized systems are merely imitations of the old manual systems, providing no more nor better information than was produced manually. The same information is merely produced by machine rather than by hand.

Management must be involved in specific steps

The steps in the development of an information system may be listed as follows:

1. Specification of goals and objectives of the system.
2. Specification of fixed system requirements.
3. Development of the system to fulfill the goals and objectives as efficiently as possible.
4. Compromise as necessary.
5. Test of the system.
6. Revision as necessary.
7. Implementation.
8. Evaluation.
9. Repeat of steps 1-8.

These are not wholly discrete steps; certainly, there will be overlap between steps. In general, however, tasks should be performed in the order indicated.

Management, on the one hand, and information technologists, on the other, must assume major responsibility for the appropriate steps in order for the system to be successful. The most important, most difficult, and most often neglected steps is the first one — specification of the goals and objectives of the system. Goals and objectives are simply other terms for what are called the outcomes of the system. In order for the final system to provide the appropriate management information, this step must be performed by management. Systems

analysis cannot possibly know what information management needs
for decision making. Only management itself can know and determine this. This step involves not merely stating information needs in general terms but specifically and in detail —
prescribing just what is needed and the time framework within
which it is needed. This is not a task that management can
perform in a few hours or even a few days. It takes a major
commitment of time and effort to determine what information
is needed for purposes of decision making.

Too often management responds to a request for systems goals
and objectives by saying, "these are the reports I have been
getting in the past — this must be what I need," or "talk to
my secretary, she knows what information I need," or "I don't
know anything about computers and information systems; you do,
so you determine what I need." Thus, in far too many cases
management abdicates its responsibility for this step, and the
systems analyst must perform it. As a result, two things
happen: the system does not adequately serve the needs of
management, and the systems analysts are accused of exceeding
their authority for systems development. Systems analysts can
assist management in the performance of this step by prodding,
making suggestions, and laying out alternatives.

Management should also perform the second step, that of
specifying the fixed system requirements. This includes determining inputs to the system and procedures which cannot be
altered — elements that must be included to comply with legal
or other requirements. These are elements that the systems
analyst cannot alter in building his system.

The third step, that of the development of the system, should
be the responsibility of systems analysts. At this stage, the
systems analysts design the input to the system and the system
procedures in such a way as to yield the goals and objectives
set by management as efficiently as possible.

The next step, that of compromise involves both management
and systems analysts. Often, the system needed to yield the
required outcomes will be too expensive or require too much
effort to implement. Thus, some compromises in the goals and
objectives must be made if the required system is to be
operated within the resources available.

All the remaining steps require a joint effort of management and systems analysts. With these steps there is not so
much danger of management assuming too much responsibility as
there is of systems analysts doing too much. Management must
be appropriately involved in each of these steps.

The needs of management at various levels

Administrators at various levels require different items
of management information. Obviously, the head of facilities
requires different information than does the head of an academic department. The president requires different information
than the vice-presidents, deans, and department heads. The
president's information needs are not satisfied by developing
information needs for the middle and lower level managers and
then providing him with all the information provided the lower
level managers. First of all, he does not need all their information in the same detail. Summaries of information provided the others will be more appropriate for him than the
detailed information. Secondly, the president requires
different information than the lower level managers. The
president must have information of a type that is not required
of anyone under him for making decisions concerning the college
as a whole.

Waste in feasibility and systems studies

Systems analysts often make detailed feasibility studies
before a decision to implement a new information system is
made. They also often make detailed studies of present systems
before developing new ones. Systems analysts seem to enjoy
drawing detailed flow charts and carefully documenting present
procedures. Both the feasibility studies and the studies of
present systems can be very expensive and time-consuming. Detailed feasibility studies, as they are usually done today,
are neither needed nor very helpful in making a decision. A
college considering a new information system would do better
to observe developed systems in similar colleges rather than
make an extensive feasibility study of its own. Besides, the

administrations's answers to certain questions — Do you want
a better information system?, Are you willing to pay for better
information?, and Are you willing to devote your own time and
the time of your staff toward the development of a better information system? — provide more information for making a
decision or whether to develop a new information system than
does extensive study.

Systems analysts are sometimes forced to spend time studying
present systems because management is unwilling to specify the
system goals and objectives, and this is the only way the
analyst can find out what needs to be done. When a computer
system is then developed, this procedure all too often results
in imitation by machine of the manual procedures, with no real
improvement in the output from the system.

Information for operations and control must be included

It is not financially feasible to develop a management
information system separate from information systems for
operations and control. Much of the information needed for
management can be obtained as a by-product of operations and
control systems. Thus the systems for the three levels —
operation, control, and management — should be developed together with the operations systems feeding information into
the control and management systems and the control system
feeding information into the management system. The operations
and control systems then form a data base from which some information for management may be drawn.

There must be coordination between departments

If each department is permitted to operate an information
system of its own independent of other departments and of the
college administration, it will not be possible to build a
management information system to meet the needs of the college
as a whole. This independent systems approach has been used
frequently. Under this approach the central information
systems or computer department is viewed as a service agency
to each department, and systems are established to meet the

complete and particular needs of each department without regard to the needs of central administration or the other
departments. If there is no central information systems or
computer department, each interested department establishes
one to fulfill its own needs. This approach is popular with
most managers of middle and lower level, who wish to operate
their own systems independent of other departments. This
approach has also resulted in excellent independent systems.
However, it results in inefficiency due to the processing of
information duplicated among departments. Of more importance,
such an approach makes it impossible to serve the needs of top
management, since information cannot be related among the
various departments as it must be in order for the needs of
top management to be served. Without central leadership,
individual department heads are not likely to coordinate their
information systems with other departments. Top management
must emphasize that information systems serve the college as
a whole — not just individual departments — and must seek
cooperation between departments for the benefit of the total
institution.

There must be a central department

In too many cases the information systems or computer
operations are assigned to one of the existing departments.
This makes it extremely difficult to serve all departments
across the campus and to develop systems to serve the needs
of management. If the information systems staff is to adequately serve all departments and top management as well, it
must be placed in the line-staff organization so that it reports directly to top management. Besides placement at the
proper level, the staff must be given responsibility and
authority for the operation of the college-wide management
information system and must have the backing of top management
in securing cooperation among departments.

Faculty members must help

The development of information systems for management decisions requires decision theory, information theory, systems

analysis, and operations research. Where specialists in these areas are available on campus, they should assist in the design of management information systems. These specialists will not have primary responsibility for the design of the system. They will merely lend technical assistance to the personnel who are responsible for the design of the system.

Justifying college management information system

At the operations level, information systems can sometimes be justified financially in terms of the cost of operating a mechanized system as compared with the cost of operating a manual system. However, at the management decision making level, the cost of producing information cannot be justified in terms of value recieved, because it is not possible to place a dollar value on management information. Improved management information should result in better management decisions, improved policies, or better plans. But no one, at this time, is able to place a dollar value on a better decision, plan, or policy. Therefore, the value of a management information system can be determined only in a subjective manner. College administrators must judge subjectively the value of management information, compare this with the cost of securing the information, and on this basis make decisions concerning the implementation of management information systems. Once the system has been established, a record of the costs of providing management information should be kept so that management can evaluate information received in terms of the cost of securing the information.

It is not possible to determine in advance all needs

The single most difficult task in the establishment of a management information system is the determination of the information needed for management decisions. It is not possible to determine in advance all the needs just as it is not possible to anticipate all the decisions that will have to be made. Management will be able to identify some specific needs. These can be accommodated in the system. However, a

system that provides only information for decisions that can
be identified in advance will not include a large amount of
information needed for unanticipated decisions. Therefore, any
management information system must be designed to provide information that can be identified in advance, to be flexible,
and to include a data base broad enough to provide for many
unanticipated requests.

The most feasible approach: a compromise

Three ways of approaching the development and implementation
of management information systems have been identified and
attempted.

Most common has been the applications approach. With this
approach one application at a time is identified, developed, and
implemented. This is done in the order of priority set by the
administration, or more commonly, in an order determined
according to the cooperation and attitude of the managers in
charge of the various applications. Thus a college may implement payroll first, then student records, facility records,
personnel records, placement, budgetary accounting, etc. The
problem with the applications approach is that, although excellent individual applications may result, an overall management information system does not result. The end product is a
group of independent applications with little opportunity for
integration into a college-wide management information system.
Such later integration is a very difficult task, perhaps more
difficult than starting from scratch. Most of the applications
will have to be changed to fit into the total system. And this
is not an easy task, both in terms of the work involved and in
terms of the feelings of the managers whose relatively new
systems must be changed.

A second approach is to design the entire information
system — operations, control, and management — in advance and
then implement it all at once. In theory this approach looks
ideal. All parts are considered and designed in advance so
all the pieces fit in place. Then they are dropped in place
together. The problem with this approach is that the task
of implementing the entire system at once is beyond the staff

and facilities resources of most colleges. As the system is
implemented so many problems occur simultaneously that chaos
results.

The third and most workable approach to the implementation of
a management information system is a combination of the two
aforementioned approaches. The overall system should be designed in advance. A priority should be established for implementation of applications based on the utility of each application
in itself and its contribution to the overall system. Then the
applications should be implemented one at a time at scheduled
intervals, with the information gaps between applications filled
in as appropriate. Thus each new application is fitted in with
present applications. Each application also contributes toward
the total system, but the task of implementation is not so mon-
umental as to be impossible.

There exist today many tools needed for the development and
implementation of improved management information systems.
Sophisticated computer hardware and software are available.
Needed knowledge and experience in the fields of information
processing, systems analysis, and operations research are also
available. Why, then, is so little progress being made toward
the development of college management information systems? The
problem lies in our inability to specify the goals and objectives
of the systems, to identify decisions that must be made, and to
specify the information needed for these decisions. The major
need for research and development in college information systems
today is not in hardware, software, or systems development. It
is in the decision process at the college level, identification
of decisions and decision situations, and specifications of
the information needed for decision making. Once the specification is fully developed, the development of information
systems to satisfy those needs can logically proceed.

[Comment by the editors. *One commentator on the paper by Mr.
Van Dusseldorp took issue with the statement that the development of management information systems requires a joint effort
of management personnel and information specialists. This
commentator argued that the decision maker and the analyst must
be one. The analyst, he said, is in a better position to make*

a decision than is the administrator, since the analyst must know what to extract from the system and for what purpose it is to be used. This is an interesting, but probably erroneous, point. Furthermore, there is within it a potential trap for the analyst. Most of us can make reasonably effective decisions if we are given adequate decision time, sufficient contact with the situation, and the time necessary for contemplation. Typically, the administrator does not operate in this kind of milieu. He is forced by the day-to-day imperatives of managing a university to make decisions in something less than an ideal context. The detachment of the analyst from the final decision process is an advantage that he should guard somewhat jealously if he is to serve his institution most effectively. His involvement in the decision making process should be primarily to provide decision-relevant information to the individuals most familiar with the total context in which the decisions must be made.]

Chapter three. Organizing for administrative-systems-analysis data processing. *John F. Chaney*

During the past decade several developments have caused colleges and universities, like industry, to become increasingly interested in improving their data-processing capabilities. These include rapid and significant growth, with an impact on all phases of operations; technological advances in data processing which make it more feasible to use techniques of systems analysis in model building and simulation, operations research, etc.; and a shift in emphasis to the external relationships with the state boards of higher education, coordinating councils, and governmental agencies.

Colleges and universities have responded to these developments principally by mechanization of well-understood clerical procedures — payroll, budget, personnel records, and student registration. But more emphasis needs to be placed on the design of information systems with provisions for institutional analysis and improved long-range planning to serve management needs. The functions involved are systems analysis, applications systems design, and programing and data-processing operations. These are the closely interrelated functions that collectively make up the "administrative systems-analysis data processing" of the title of this chapter.

This chapter is addressed to considerations which will help provide an organizational structure conducive to the use of major technological advances and methodology. It first directs attention to the administrative-systems-analysis data-processing organization and its relationships to college and university operations. Second, it directs attention to the administrative-systems-analysis data-processing function in an organizational structure which will accommodate emerging methodologies, e.g., operations research, mathematical methods to aid decision making, modeling, and institutional analysis. Third, it directs attention to methods and concepts intended to provide a check list of important considerations and principles for organizing

administrative-systems-analysis data-processing. Fourth, it
directs attention to the future and offers orientation toward
an organizational structure that will accommodate new technology and its influence on the interrelationship of functional
operating data systems.

Technological advances

Technological advances have improved the capability for use
of a variety of management-science techniques. These capabilities and trends will affect the organization of administrative-
systems-analysis data-processing and will play an increasingly
important role in the organization, as the functions are
identified as belonging to management.

The evolution of the computer has been dramatic. Today's
electronic computer will perform computations several million
times faster than the 1944 Harvard Mark I. There has been an
accompanying decrease in computing costs — of a magnitude of
several thousand times less to execute a particular solution
to a problem. There is no foreseeable end to this trend in
the fourth generation of computers now on the drawing boards.
Three generations of computers in a short time have provided
a technology with many implications other than reduced costs
of computation. For example, functions previously not econom-
ically or technically feasible, such as storing masses of
historical data, are now available.

Storage capability removes the previous, confounding
restraint of limited-size records. Records may now be of any
size — though there may be some practical, economic limitations.

Teleprocessing capability (permitting user on-line operations, data entry at the point and time of creation, information
display for the user on an as-needed basis, etc.) will bring
the user closer to his data and do much to relieve the lack of
responsiveness inherent in many batch-processing operations.

The emerging computer utility with a large, central computer
serving many users through input-output terminals, connected by
data communications lines, may have an impact on the computer
acquisition question. The small college or university will
have to demonstrate that its processing needs can be satisfied

at comparatively low initial costs before funds will be
willingly expended for local facilities.

The evolution of the data-processing function

The way in which the administrative-systems-analysis data-
processing function has evolved and been placed organizationally
is closely related to the evolution of the computer and technological change. The most common pattern was a tabulating department that was first to use the equipment. This department
absorbed the application-systems design function to create a
data-processing function; it reported at about the fifth
organizational level. A second pattern was similar except
that the application-systems design function absorbed the
tabulating function. Third, two organizations developed —
one for data-processing operations and one for systems design
— with no assurance that the two would report to the same
management. Fourth, a department evolved for all the related
functions of systems analysis, application-systems design, and
data processing, with the director reporting at the second or
third level of management.

In the first three patterns of organization, application-
systems design and data-processing tend to remain at a low
level. Management tends to say they are important, but there
is evidence of routine treatment and cases in which they are
almost ignored. Systems are generally limited to routine
clerical operations, and most activities involve the conversion
to mechanized solutions rather than higher-level projects.

In the fourth pattern of organization the highly related
functions of systems analysis, application-systems design,
and programing and data-processing operations (in our terms,
"administrative-systems-analysis data-processing") involve
many phases of the institution's activities, cutting across
functional lines and involving the interrelationships of
information flow between departments. A department of this
type receives management's attention and involvement. Attention
is given to placement in the institution where the operations
can best serve all departments and all levels of management.
Moves to place these functions at a high organizational level

are motivated by a common goal: to place them in an organizational position where they will develop minimum departmental biases so they will serve the broader needs of the institution as well as specific operating functions. Where such a placement has been made, it generally means that a high-level administrator understands the significance of computer-based information systems and wants to make sure that these functions are applied to higher-level projects.

The principal functions of administrative data processing

There are three principal functions of administrative data processing.

1. The first function is the design and development of application systems or systems of transactional type which encompass requirements specified by the user. These requirements are often referred to by the data processor as the "problem definition."

There are difficulties in dealing with problem definition. The user is hard pressed to specify his needs, because he cannot predict all the information he will need several years from now. For this reason and sometimes because he does not do a thorough job of planning, the definition may be incomplete and lead to additional work. Fear of the latter sometimes causes the data processor to confront the decision maker with such statements as "Make sure you've told me of all the data we need to collect and all the reports you desire as output. Changes are expensive; we won't be able to reprogram this again next year." As a result, many managers want reporting systems which display every possible combination of information conceivable. Systems become overcomplex and therefore unresponsive to changing needs.

The user too often believes he cannot state his requirements because he does not understand the technical problems of data processing. The technicalities should be relatively unimportant to the user, and he should rely on the data processor for the technical solutions. The user should define analytical processes (the general computational or associative scheme not related to technicalities which are a function of machine processing) to support his requirements. The user should prepare

complete and understandable nonmachine statements establishing
the analytical procedures by which his data are collected,
categorized, manipulated, and maintained. He should distin-
guish between details which are simply a function of characteristics of programing and machines and details which are
basic to the actual analytical functions affected by computer
programs.

The user should not be expected to be an expert in technical
matters of data processing; however, he should be well ac-
quainted with the fundamental systems and computer programs
which support them so that he can verify that the systems do,
in fact, conform to the analytical requirements.

2. The second function is programing and program maintenance
for the application system, designed to satisfy user requirements. Program maintenance refers to the work involved in
keeping the programs current to meet changing requirements of
the system or changing computer technology.

3. The third function is operations. These will not be
discussed in this paper.

*Two terms defined: "systems analysis" and "application-systems
design"*

At first in data-processing technology, the term "systems
analysis" described the responsibilities assigned to a person
for working with users in the study of a system of transactional
type which was to be mechanized. Requirements were determined,
a system of programs was designed, and computer programs were
written and implemented. These responsibilities might better
be described and understood under the term "application-systems
design."

"Systems analysis" is now also used to describe the responsibilities associated with higher-level systems-analysis
studies. The latter include the activities necessary to un-
tangle a variety of complex conditions and reduce them to
understandable terms to help the decision maker by furnishing
measures of effectiveness, costs, and implications of alternative courses of action. These studies may be very complex,
involving the use of operations research, industrial engineering

techniques, models, and simulation. They may involve determination of requirements for a completely new system in which
there is no experience or in the implementation of information
systems, and so on.

"Administrative-systems analysis" refers to higher-level
systems studies, as described above, while "application-
systems design" is included as a function of data-processing.
The relationship of administrative-systems analysis and data
processing has been given little attention in higher education.
Since the functions are closely related, these two activities
should be together administratively to provide capabilities
which complement each other. The data-processing function of
design and development of application systems or systems of
transactional type is performed by systems people who, in
general, do not perform administrative-systems analysis. The
principal reasons for this are the lack of training in the
necessary techniques, lack of mathematical background, and a
difference in frames of reference as conditioned by formal
training and experience. The application-systems design com-
plements the higher-level administrative-systems analysis
because it supplies data for modeling and simulation, operations
research, and so on. Administrative alignment enhances the
capability for design of interrelated systems which provide
a capability for management information systems to which the
application-systems designer, for user's systems, and the
systems analyst, for higher-level systems, will apply their
talents. The computer is a supporting tool; however, it is
only one center of attention in the data-processing function.

A definite weakness exists in the lack of interchange and
cooperation between the systems analyst for higher-level systems, who professes to be on the cutting edge of developing
management information systems and models, and the data processor. Two attitudes seem to be prevalent. The model builder
takes the position that the data processors are just a service
group who have nothing to do with problems of these kinds; yet
they design and operate functional data systems — students,
staff, space, budget — which contain data essential to successful model building and implementation. The data processor
often views the model builder (usually on a grant) as a theorist

going through an academic exercise not likely to become an
administrative production system of use to the institution,
basing his work on contrived data and which will not provide
a practical solution for management use. It does appear that
the latter is not the best methodology, and neither is the
development of data-processing systems with no objectives for
institutional analysis and use of models. The data processor
and the model builder are important to each other and if
brought together will complement each other.

The effective use of data depends on an ability to analyze
relationships and present alternative courses of action to
policy makers. This analytical ability is of a high level
generally found in the systems analyst with a background in
systems engineering and management sciences. His analytical
effectiveness and ability to interpret are enhanced if he is
associated with the data in design phases of systems development and if he is familiar with the data-processing system.

Role in policy making

Administrative-systems-analysis data-processing is supportive
in nature, i.e., it does not establish policy. The functions
of the university are carried out through responsibilities
assigned to organizational units and policies associated with
the assigned responsibilities. The registrar, bursar, space
office, office responsible for institutional analysis, etc.,
have assigned functions for which they are responsible. However, the interaction with higher-level systems analysis is
not always clear, and to the extent that it is not, the effect
on policy is not clear.

The way in which management chooses to use administrative-
systems-analysis data-processing support services has much to
do with the way in which policy is affected, since management
objectives are reflected in the kind of systems implemented.
For example, in student scheduling, the philosophy that students
should be given choice of section, time, and instructor determines the system structure. The policy of student choice,
which is the objective of management, is therefore implemented
by administrative-systems-analysis data-processing. These

functions are used as a management tool when higher-level
management defines information-systems controls, objectives,
and goals to be implemented, systems which tend to be of the
control and strategic type. Administrative-systems-analysis
data-processing brings together the transactional-system needs
of a user and the overall need of control, or strategic-
information systems, to serve the objectives of higher-level
management — all of which involve coordinated development and
processing. The administrative-systems-analysis data processing
functions used in this way contribute to the development and
implementation of policy.

A function of the higher-level systems-analysis group is to
join the user requirements and management policy objectives,
which may not be the same. The use of management sciences —
e.g., models, simulation, and operations research methodologies
— to support resource allocations is related to establishing
and implementing management philosophies in operational systems.
It is possible that systems analysis will prove influential
through capabilities if providing a variety of alternative
solutions to management problems and will thereby enter into
the policy-making process.

Planning and management for the proper organizational level

The organization of administrative-systems analysis data
processing should not necessarily be bound by an existing
traditional function nor changed without strong reasons. The
combined functions should report to top management. New information-systems technology requires new solutions to old and
new problems and a relaxing of old constraints, best attained
through the commitment of top management. Such a commitment
will provide systems development for all levels of operations,
as well as systems design from inception, to support management's use in the allocation of resources, internal management,
and long-range planning.

Although not as apparent in higher education, there is a
gradual trend in business to locate these functions at a higher
level in the organization. Locating data processing in a
parochial department creates the possibility, if not the

probability, that the computer will be used principally for
that department's function at the expense of others and ultimately at the expense of institution-wide information systems.
It places the facility in a subsidiary position, making it
more difficult for other departments to have access to the
computer. Quite aside from these possibilities, the overall
view of the institution and the standardization and configuration for information systems supported by the computer can be
more effectively achieved if the facility reports at a high
level.

   Planning. Organizing for administrative-systems-analysis
data-processing must include provisions for more attention to
planning objectives and programs (in a program budget sense),
effective management, centralization versus decentralization,
and a number of other considerations.

   In many organizations too little attention has been given
to specifying the objectives and supporting programs, projects,
and tasks within the overall objectives of the institution.
In some instances, institutional objectives may not be spelled
out, and in others, no attempt has been made to establish the
relationships.

   To illustrate the structure of a "PPBS-like" system which
can be used internally to monitor, control, and direct efforts,
while at the same time communicating direction to other units
and management for review and coordination, let us define and
identify four major elements.

   1. Objectives: These are statements of the overall goals to
be attained. They are not limited to administrative-systems-
analysis data-processing objectives, but rather are a reflec-
tion of the institutional objectives from the viewpoint of
this organization. Subobjectives must be consistent with the
more global objectives, as must those of related offices.
Not included in this category are institutional objectives to
which these functions make no direct or significant contribution. A comprehensive program statement indicates that these
objectives are to be coordinated with other departments involved.

   2. Programs: These are a collection of subprojects and
activities undertaken by various offices directed toward

attaining the above objectives. Here again, programs are not
limited to administrative-systems-analysis data-processing
alone; they may involve other departments. These programs
reflect administrative-systems-analysis data-processing's
involvement and are thus a subset of the totality of all
institutional programs; but again, they imply a direct and
significant involvement. They must also be coordinated with
other departments.

3. Projects: These consist of a set of tasks and are the
responsibility of administrative-systems-analysis data-processing. These projects, together with those defined by other
organizational units, collectively support the programs.

4. Tasks: Projects are broken down into tasks which are the
center of activity.

Objectives. Let us list here objectives:

(1) Improve the institution's information systems.
   (a) Improve responsiveness in providing data-processing
       and analytical support to the various organizational
       units of the institution.
   (b) Bring the user closer to the information needed —
       that is, develop flexibility and shorten lead times
       relative to information requests.
(2) Contribute to improved planning capacity of the institution.
(3) Develop methods for more effective allocation of the in-
    stitution's resources.
(4) Institute more efficient and economical ways to utilize
    the computing facilities and staff of data-processing, and
    simultaneously improve services.
(5) Improve management decision-making capabilities.

Programs. Examples of programs include:

(1) Coordinate, design, install, and maintain institution-wide
    administrative data systems at the proposal stage, in
    development phases, and in production.
(2) Do PPBS design and development: design and develop a
    system to support long-range planning.
(3) Evaluate hardware; recommend configurations and acquisi-
    tions.

(4) Develop documentation standards; establish and maintain documentation; develop code control and assignment guidelines; establish and maintain master code books.

(5) Support, develop, and implement operations-research applications.

(6) Support, develop, and implement institutional modeling and analyses.

(7) Educate and train in data processing, operations research, and systems analysis.

The need for improved management. Several factors contribute to the lack of planning for administrative-system-analysis data-processing. Departments have been established without a definition of the scope of their responsibilities. Relatively low-level placement of the facility in the institution has prevented securing a management-caliber director capable of higher-level planning. Directors have been taken from the technical ranks, i.e., from among the most proficient and possibly most experienced programers and systems analysts. The man with less technical skill and more management awareness is rejected because of the technical priority required by some problem at hand. The feeling prevails that another "generalist" or "management type" to run the organization is not needed, but rather a "technical type" to get the job at hand done. Too often the director is in the operational line "putting out fires" and simply does not have the time for planning.

Administrative-systems-analysis data-processing is expensive. If a computer is used successfully, there is inevitably a trend to replace it with a larger and more expensive one or add another. Thus, it requires management in a stricter sense than some other facilities. Forecasting the use of this facility is difficult because realized use is controlled by the funds made available rather than by need. Need is always far in excess of capacity; therefore, capacity controls the amount of computation. Nevertheless, planning and forecasting are an extremely important part of the rational growth of the institution's use. Plans should be developed several years ahead (even though long-range forecasts will not always be very accurate), with a yearly cycle dealing with the short-range need and adjustment of resources.

There is an inclination in institutions to shy away from
the word "management." However, the cost of these functions,
together with (1) fear that they are not being used with maximum effectiveness, (2) lack of understanding of how resources
are being spent and how they can be controlled, and (3) the
effect on a great many people in different ways (intense
rivalry for control, complaints and misunderstandings damaging
to effective use and thus to the institution as a whole) demand
that higher-level management be assured the functions are being
run fairly for all parties concerned. Sound management is required no matter how the users react.

The director. The person who has primary responsibility
for the administrative-systems-analysis data-processing function
must be of management caliber, yet respected for his technical
ability and ability to discuss data processing in terms that
users understand. He must be able to communicate effectively
with all levels of management and to present his ideas in a
way that wins cooperation and support from operating management.
His technical competence is important, but he must be capable
of building and managing a professional staff of high caliber
and with many diverse talents (systems engineers, operations
researchers, industrial engineers, application-systems designers, programers, computer operators). He needs to establish effective communications with line management, administer many diverse, complex projects, and motivate the staff.
All this requires ability of a high order. The demands are
such that he must be able to work effectively under continual
pressure. The director must desire that the function be run
to the satisfaction of the academic community, of users, and
of the administration. Very broad responsibility — say, high-
level policy decisions — may be vested in a policy committee,
but day-to-day interpretations of policy must be made with
authority, must be made quickly, and require an experienced
person with a good understanding of university administrative
operations.

Centralization versus decentralization

The issue of centralization versus decentralization should not be ignored in a study of organizational relationships. Much has been said on numerous occasions and in many different ways. Three principal arrangements seem to exist: several users, each with his own facility; a central facility for administrative use only; and a central facility for instruction, research, and administrative use.

In the opinion of this author, a central facility for administrative use only is the best arrangement, for two principal reasons: (1) There is a need for information systems resulting from interrelated data systems (the capability for bringing together data for comprehensive analysis of staff, space, students, facilities, and budget). This concept assumes that each segment of the system can interrelate with the other segments for easy access to data requirements from one or a number of other segments.[1] (2) There are serious constraints imposed by differences in types of people attracted to different types of work and differences in the use of equipment when instruction, research, and administrative uses are combined in a central facility.

There are many other considerations, including these:

1. The rigid schedule requirements of administrative systems require a severe priority discipline.
2. Continuous program maintenance and modification are required of dynamic administrative systems.
3. There are numerous users and people affected by the output of administrative systems.
4. Data responsibility is important to each research user, for each is responsible for his own data.
5. There may be divergent orientations imposed on analytical and programing staff for scientific as contrasted with administrative systems.
6. Administrative job set-ups may call for great variety (numerous input files, intermediate check-point balances, custom multipart forms output), while the job stream of student or research problems may be continuous.

7. Computer-science research may influence operations. The computer facility may itself be the object of research — appropriately so, for benefits of new technology should accrue to the university — and therefore be subject to modification. The result may be an unreliable operation from the viewpoint of the administrative user.
8. Problems may arise of priority of utilization, as scientific and administrative uses expand at different rates toward facility saturation.
9. Analysis and development of administrative systems generally require (a) consensus among many users, (b) resolution of incomplete statements of requirements, and (c) understanding of complex man-machine relationships such as student registration.
10. Management decisions based on hardware cost alone do not include dimensions of software, e.g., user consulting services, applications development, and personnel. A narrow view is dangerous.
11. It may be worthwhile to consider decentralizing facilities, with centralized management.
12. The principal thrust, whether serving academic uses or administrative uses, places severe constraints on combined operations.
13. There may be a question of the adequacy of service from the viewpoint of convenience and timeliness.

The small college

In the institutional setting used as a frame of reference for this paper — the large university — goals have been presented which will be difficult for the small college to achieve — for example, the position that a central facility for administrative use only is the best arrangement. Though best, it is not realistic for a small college. In the nation's 2,500 and more institutions of higher education, as of January 1, 1969, only an estimated 1,100 had computer facilities of any kind available for use by their faculty and students.[2] If a computer is available at all, there may be no choice but to coordinate the three functions of instruction, research,

and administration. In these instances, a great deal of
attention needs to be given to the administrative arrangements
whereby a balance is achieved between the administrative and
academic functions.

The small college may look to six approaches to gain access
to a computer facility: (1) use of a computer off-campus, (2)
use of remote terminals from computers at a university or
commercial time-sharing center, (3) cooperative use of a small
computer with other colleges (by means other than communication
lines), (4) use of an independent small computer in each
college, (5) cooperative use of small to medium computer
communication system, and (6) use of a small computer as a
stand-alone system or as a terminal.[3]

Future developments

Continuing developments will have an important effect on
the organization of administrative-systems-analysis data processing. Undoubtedly, many are unknown; however, some seem
clear.

Administrative-systems-analysis data-processing requirements
will increase due to the number of new applications to be
developed and increasing volumes of current applications. Of
these the higher-level projects will receive more attention.

The skill required by current technology is much less than
will be required in the future. Personnel with high-level
capabilities must be developed.

The sophistication (knowledge and education) of users will
continue to increase, and as a result so will demands for the
use of information systems for control and decision making and
a greater degree of participation in systems analysis, design,
and the like.

Plans must exist to build-in flexibility and adaptability
so as to utilize new software, hardware, and concepts. Those
in use today will become past generation, and it is necessary
to devote considerable attention to planning for new developments.

Conversion efforts are increasingly more costly. More
attention must be given to future developments to avoid un-
necessary allocation of resources to this activity.

The development of institution-wide systems must be studied further to avoid redundant effort and to assure their effective utilization.

The trend toward the use of information for policy formulation will continue to increase in the future. Therefore, the capability to interrelate data systems to support institutional planning and management through a set of uniformly coded data elements must be a prime concern.

Managers of the future will be solidly grounded in computer uses through early education and will utilize computer technology as a common tool.

Systems planners and those who manage systems must develop an increasing awareness of the needs of high-level management.

The need for uniting various areas to resolve information-systems problems will receive greater recognition. Systems planners, operations research specialists, application-systems designers, and data processing personnel should work together as a team from the inception of a project through the cycle of systems analysis, problem definition, application-systems design, programing, and production implementation. Skills in various scientific techniques such as mathematical programing and model building provide an analytical, problem-solving capability to management in complex decision-making situations. Skills in the development and installation of source-data acquisition systems, data transmission, and computer systems are providing application-systems solutions for functional operating systems. Computers, as a tool of scientific-problem solving and functional systems operations, are run by skilled operations personnel. The relationship between these specialists seems obvious in a high-level department which will unite their activities while maintaining the identify of special techniques.

Notes

1. John F. Chaney, "Data Management and Interrelated Data
      Systems for Higher Education," WICHE-ACE Seminar, April
      1969.

2. John W. Hamblen, "The Small College and the Computer,"
   Educational Media, vol. 1 (April 1969), pp. 5-7.
3. Ibid.

Chapter four. The organization, economics, and allocation of resources to administrative systems analysis.   *Martin L. Zeigler*

Within the recent past, national attention has been dramatically focused on higher education. Dissatisfaction expressed by students, and in some quarters by faculty, has been augmented by public criticism of the higher educational establishment. Unprecedented enrollments and rising costs have given pause to university decision makers and to legislatures, especially in the public sector. Increasing enrollments have also created dilemmas for decision makers in the private sector of higher education. Although there has been a tradition in that sector of providing quality education without public aid, this philosophy seems to be changing rapidly. Thus, the demand for resources in support of higher education has reached an all-time record and is continuing to rise. As a consequence, university managers are being pressured to obtain more data in order to make effective decisions and to justify their actions.

In order to achieve a higher level of justification for program support, an increasing number of decision makers are turning to administrative-systems analysis in the expectation that it will help to provide viable answers. The emphasis is on the development of goals and objectives from which a conceptual framework can be derived and the resource requirements of the institution better identified. In addition, it is expected that administrative systems analysis will make it possible to anticipate the consequences of alternate policy decisions. Despite the promise which some of the newer and more exotic methodologies hold, the surface has barely been scratched in the use of these techniques. Substantial efforts will have to be made in order to develop such systems to a point where they can provide the necessary information to allow institutional decision makers at all levels to effectively administer programs.

It is not the purpose of this chapter to treat the funda-
mentals of systems analysis but rather to view them within the
context of their relevance to decision makers and others who
will use these systems in higher education.

The role of management

University management personnel are constantly faced with a
variety of alternatives for the application of scarce resources.
Historically, our information systems have not been adequate to
analyze the competing needs of the institution. Consequently,
too often policies have grown like topsy rather than being designed to reach specified goals. With the advent of systems
analysis, it is incombent upon management to think through the
goals and objectives of the institution systematically and to
use such tools for better planning than has been possible in
the past.

A distinction should be drawn between management and administrative personnel. The former are charged with the responsibility to formulate policy and to make decisions which
may have significant effect upon the direction of an institution. Valid decisions are usually best made when management
has available enough information to adequately assess alternatives. On the other hand, administrative personnel may be
viewed as implementers of policy decisions. It is they who
deal with day-to-day operations and also provide information
required by management.

The relative importance of various university activities
does change. For this reason the university structure must
remain plastic and have the capacity to anticipate the changing
values and needs of our society, and university objectives must
be constantly reevaluated and restated. Such modifications,
however, do not necessarily imply a revision in programs, nor
should it be inferred that reallocation of university resources
is always necessary. But through a constant monitoring of programs with modern systems techniques, administrators are in a
sounder position to effect changes when they are necessary.

The lack of viable information systems in the past has
created a disjointed situation in which management at different

levels of the structure has based its decisions and recommendations on completely different sets of imputs and outputs. This
has caused conflicts, particularly when decisions affirmed at
one level had to be overruled at another. Only through modern
administrative systems is it possible to make available consistent information to all levels of management, including the
feedback which can be used for adjustments in subsequent decisions.

One of the major frustrations facing university administrators
has been the lack of interfacing between the systems of respective offices. The result of this weakness has been inconsistencies in the information necessary for decision making.
Such inconsistencies place management on the horns of a dilemma:
What sets of information should be used in making decisions?
A simple case will illustrate the problem. In order to gain
understanding of resource utilization and requirements, the
decision maker requests information from the offices of institutional research, the registrar, and space. To his dismay,
he learns that none of the figures agree. Further, in his
discussions with the head of the department in question, he
gains the impression that the latter does not agree with any
of the other three.

There are usually sound reasons for these differences, at
least from the viewpoints of the heads of the respective offices.
However, the disparity often baffles the decision maker and
tends to erode confidence. Thus the final outcome in this
situation is likely to be based on pure negotiation. The
tragedy in the case is that too often debates are centered on
data rather than the merit of the program. (It should be noted
that even where sound administrative systems are implemented,
negotiation will still play a prominent role in the decision
making process, for there are always alternatives, and frequently, value judgments will influence final decisions.)

There are several other sources of frustration which beset
management:

a. Overselling on the part of vendors and systems personnel.
   In their efforts to promote a product, vendors have
   implied product potential which simply could not be

realized either as quickly or as easily as management
was led to believe.

b. Displacement or lack of clarity in the establishment of
priorities. The result is that systems personnel pro-
liferate the energies they apply to priorities which they
have set and which may not meet the needs of management.

c. Time span required to develop, write, and test programs,
together with program inflexibility, e.g., a minor change
in requirements necessitating major program changes. The
newly developed general information-systems programing is
alleged to be the answer to this problem.

These are a few of the problems which management encounters
in its efforts to use administrative systems. But it would be
unreasonable to indict systems personnel alone. As a partial
solution, management at some institutions has sought to re-
organize and engage staff specialists. This point will be
amplified later.

As mentioned above, institutions must be sensitive to the
changing needs of society and the resultant impact upon
institutional programs. Thus, it is essential that constant
monitoring of programs be continued. The study of trends is
useful. Is a program on the incline or decline? Should more
resources be allocated to a program which seems to be faltering?
Is there a need for change in the structure? Systems analysis
can be immensely useful to the decision maker, as he charts the
course for an institution, by providing him with an understanding of the trends and alternatives which may be considered
in the decision making process. To be of the most utility to
university authorities the trends must be related to the total
resources which are required by a program. Too frequently, the
manager is forced to make decisions based upon the knowledge
of parts of the total program. Through effective systems
analysis a composite can be forged which will allow him to
analyze policy alternatives systematically.

The value of an administrative system is dependent upon how
effectively it can be implemented and how well information can
be fed back to decision makers. In a system that functions
properly a large number of people will be involved. These

are located not only within the administrative-systems group
but also in related offices throughout the university. Since
the system permeates the entire structure, the cooperation of
these people is essential. Any change that is imposed affects
the lives of these people, who have been in positions of responsibility for varying lengths of time and who may have some
rather crystallized ideas about the way their work should be
accomplished. Consequently, pockets of resistance created by
senior executives or even low-grade clerks may be encountered
by the systems groups. This does not imply any sense of dis-
loyalty to the institution on their part but rather suggests
that change requires time, not only to develop a system but
to effectively implement it.

One way that change can be expedited is by a clear statement of the goals and objectives for the institution as well
as for each of the operating offices. Beyond that, the doors
of communication must be kept constantly open, and a training
program must be evolved. Such measures will diminish the
number of misconceptions and the fears of those who think they
may be displaced. The following is a case in point. The
principal responsibility of a budget analyst was to be sure that
accurate records were kept as new positions were opened or funds
were transferred from one line item to another. When it came
time to systematize the budget, this individual resisted the
idea and suggested that only a state of chaos would exist if
such a change were made. It later developed that he was concerned about his own future welfare. After he learned that he
would be relieved of the detailed transcribing, but would still
be held accountable for the accuracy of the information, he
became cooperative. Personnel must be constantly assured that
systems help them fulfill their responsibilities.

The role of the user

It might be argued that all persons and offices which draw
upon administrative systems are "users." But the term in this
context identifies a line office — e.g., the registrar. His
primary responsibilities are to register students and to
maintain adequate records for them. Because his office is

intimately engaged in an activity upon which management decisions may be based, at least in part, it is important to
consider the role of such an office and how it might function
within a system. The role of the user is twofold: (a) to meet
day-to-day operational needs and (b) to support analytical
systems. In addition, the registrar's function pervades many
activities of the university structure. Although the goals
and objectives of the office may seem to be simple and straightforward, a more detailed analysis of the tasks and workloads
involved suggests otherwise. The development of a statement
of objectives is a challenge in itself for most registrars,
and indeed, for most systems people who have had experience in
that area. Reference to the registrar's office is merely
illustrative of a single user type. More important and more
complex is the interfacing of several user type offices.

Much has been said about the need for problem definition.
This is an age-old dilemma, and it is certainly a source of
irritation between systems personnel and systems users. Systems
personnel will frequently attempt to define the problem for
the user. This simplified approach often leads to disputes
between the user and the systems people, growing partly out
of their inability to fully comprehend each others needs and
interests. While the user has not systematically defined his
problem himself, he may accuse the systems personnel of trying
to run his shop when they do so. To some extent it may be
argued that he has a case, for it is true that systems people
have had to make decisions. Choices are selected from among
alternatives, and on some occasions these choices are made
without benefit of user consultation. Under these conditions,
the user may refuse to implement the system, because it does
not meet what he sees as his requirements.

These weaknesses in interfacing can be resolved, at least
to some extent, by the formation of a users group (including
administrative systems personnel) which meets on a regular
basis to discuss the requirements for each of the offices.
This group should be appointed by the senior executive officer
of the institution and should be composed of representatives
from each of the user offices, including teaching units, and
a faculty member. The primary purpose is to develop plans and

procedures for effecting better cooperation among the major
administrative offices of the university for the flow and
analysis of institutional data. Such a group also serves as a
forum for review of systems definition, provided by the user,
and systems solution, provided by the implementer, to assure
those concerned that needs at all levels will be met. As an
institution moves toward the development of comprehensive
administrative systems and improved programs for processing
data in relation to institutional planning and decision making,
it becomes increasingly necessary that communication and
coordination among the major administrative offices be effectively maintained. The users group can provide the means for
interchange of information concerning proposed procedural
changes within an office, especially in cases in which it may
affect the information required by another office.

Weaknesses in interfacing can be resolved, at least to some
extent, by such regular group meetings. Meetings of this kind
not only stimulate communication between systems personnel and
users but also create an atmosphere in which they assist in
solving the problems of one another. Furthermore, redundancies
are less likely to occur throughout the system when people are
kept informed of what others are doing. As users learn the
needs of other users they begin to comprehend the systems requirements, not only for their own purposes, but for the
institution.

After the vehicle for communication has been established
among the users and administrative-systems personnel, the matter
of problem definition becomes easier. It is also easier to
establish priorities. With an arrangement such as this, the
users are frequently less parochial, and they participate more
freely in the establishment of priorities. Hence, systems
personnel are more likely to be supported in decisions which
need to be made for the development of sound practices.

An additional advantage of a users group is that it provides
thrust for the development of new systems. Although much impetus comes from the lower ranks, the unique composition of such
a group — chaired by an executive and composed of heads of user
offices — provides an opportunity for developmental thrust to
emanate from any level.

Organization of administrative systems

Considerable attention should be given to the way in which an administrative systems group is organized. While it is clear that communications are important between users and the systems group, internal communications between members of systems personnel are even more important. Systems personnel may become segmented even among executive officers. The theoretically oriented model builders, who engage in the art of conceptualizing an institution, may be located in a quite different spot in the hierarchy from those who deal with the translation of models into operating systems. Sometime data-processing personnel are divorced from systems people. Yet all these activities and functions are interrelated and should be centralized administratively to facilitate supervision and cooperation.

Model builders have distinctly different backgrounds from those who develop operating systems, and they are distinguishable from personnel who deal with operating data systems and data processing in the traditional sense. As one example, most people who engage in model building and simulation have advanced college degrees, whereas those who maintain the operating data systems may be high-school or at best junior-college graduates. Thus, not only may there be a wide disparity between ability levels, but frames of reference may also vary markedly. Internal communication among the systems group can be facilitated if the various segments are combined under one director.

Communications can and do break down not only within but also between offices. Breakdown often occurs between resource-analysis offices. Some institutions are attempting to solve the communication gap between such offices (e.g., budget, institutional research, administrative systems, and space) by organizing them under one executive officer. Such an officer usually serves in a staff capacity. Since he has no line authority, the possibility of conflict of interest — between his own sphere of responsibility and the requirements of the total institution — is reduced.

As institutions become more complex, the staff function grows in its significance. Decision makers must rely on such personnel

to interrelate information, to reduce volumes of data to
manageable proportions, and to provide defensible alternatives.
When resource analysis offices are coordinated as outlined above,
greater team effort and cooperation usually result.

Selection of a director

The director of an administrative systems group will serve
in a pivotal position within the university structure. He
should be the spokesman for the administrative-systems group.
To function effectively his background and training will need
to be unique. He should be knowledgeable about the latest tools
of operations analysis and about human relations.

As much care should be devoted to the selection of a director
as is given to evaluation and selection of an academic department
head. The relative success and progress of an academic department is largely dependent upon the vigor and imagination of its
head. The same might be said of administrative systems. The
director will need to provide direction for the systems group
from the most complex conceptualizations to the resolutions of
common, mundane, and everyday problems of operations. Furthermore, he will need to be in constant communication with the
user groups if he is to continue to enjoy their respect and
support.

What are the costs?

The direct dollar costs of an administrative-systems installation can be determined with little difficulty. As a general
rule of thumb, the hardware costs for a computer installation
will be approximately one-half of the total cost required to
underwrite the operation. From a management viewpoint, it is
essential to have some sound knowledge about the magnitude of
the commitment which must be made. Yet the strength of the
commitment, in sound management systems, to facilitate decision
making should be measured against the institutional objectives
which are influenced by internal and external forces. Furthermore, the requirements of extramural agencies may be such that
it might be less expensive to implement such a system than to

struggle along with outdated methods. A simple example will
illustrate this point.

Assume that a state coordinating board for higher education
requests all institutions to participate in a cost study. The
methodologies and procedures which are to be followed have been
worked out by institutional representatives in collaboration
with representatives from the board of higher education. Certainly the need for sound systems analysis is obvious. It
would be fatuous indeed for the institution to shirk its
responsibilities and not provide the kind of information requested: such shirking could result in serious reduction of
fund support. The point is that despite high costs — the
development and implementation of cost studies can be
expensive — the return far exceeds the investment. To put it
simply, what does it cost *not* to implement the activity?

In general, institutions seem not to have given a high
priority to cost considerations in the initial support and
development of administrative systems. There are several reasons for this. If the objectives of the institution and of
the users were not clearly defined, the magnitude of the
commitment was never carefully considered. The magnitude of
the workload may also have been such that it could not be
handled by other means. As can be seen from the illustration
cited above, a complex institution obviously could not conduct
a comprehensive cost study without relatively sophisticated
administrative systems personnel. Yet it should not be inferred
that there are no ways in which costs can be measured. Certainly units of output can be identified, and costs can be
assigned to them.

The payoff of an administrative-systems division is long-
range in nature, for it is through the development of articulated
systems that management is able to make sounder decisions regarding the allocation of resources. The chief academic officer
is often faced with the question of whether he should allocate
an additional faculty member to a teaching department or
whether he should authorize a new position for an administrative
office. Until our systems are more adequately defined and
developed, managers will continue to search for solutions and
to make them on the basis of the best (or the only) information

which they have available. Systems analysis will aid management in making such fundamental decisions. It is only through
the implementation of these systems that policy alternatives
can be systematically viewed and the cost of each alternative
analyzed in light of relative benefits.

In summary, the direct dollar costs can be easily determined.
Additional costs, which may be substantial, can be determined
only after management decides what it wishes to accomplish.
Subsequent to that decision, analysis of total manpower needs
for all affected offices can be derived and approximate total
costs estimated.

What are the benefits?

Several benefits accrue to decision makers as a result of
the implementation of administrative-systems analysis.

Sounder internal management. Because systems analysis makes
it possible for decision makers to have good information related
to available resources, they are in a sounder position to select from among alternative policy decisions. They can anticipate the consequences of decisions and (assuming that the
information is properly aligned) how decisions may affect
programs. Furthermore, pertinent information can be made
available to all levels of management, not only facilitating
but stimulating planning and analysis of the use of resources.

Consistency in outside reports. Unless data systems are
appropriately interfaced, there is a significant risk that
inconsistent reports may be submitted to outside agencies.
Evolution of sound administrative systems will prevent that
unhappy situation, since the same information will be carried
through to all points within the system.

Reduction in overlap of offices. A clear statement of the
goals and objectives for the institution as a whole provides
a framework within which it is possible for each office to
formulate its own plans. Good planning should enable each
office to discharge its responsibilities without creating a

void within the system, while minimizing possible overlaps of effort.   Moreover, a clearer definition of goals, which provides a sound frame of reference with which an office can identify, eases possible diffusion of responsibilities.

Definition of problems.   Effective definition of a problem — in other words, what the user wants — is a constant perturbation. However, clarification of goals and objectives of the user will assist systems personnel in providing the kind of information needed.   The user should also be in a better position to describe his needs, since he is aware of the tasks he is expected to perform.

Office identity.   Directors and supervisors of units sometimes resist the implementation of effective systems, especially those which are interfaced with other offices, principally because of a fear of the loss of information control and identity. Indeed, fears may not be entirely without foundation, inasmuch as systems analysis has, from time to time, indicated that certain offices were redundant.   On the other hand, there have been cases where the need for augmentation to fill voids which had not been previously identified has been shown by such analysis.

Major changes coming

The rest of this chapter will be devoted to changes which are either now being implemented or looming on the horizon. Management people already have an increased awareness of administrative systems if for no other reason than their growing knowledge of the sheer magnitude of costs associated with the support of such programs.   Some time ago, a burdened university executive was overheard to exclaim that there are three things in a university which can absorb all available resources: libraries, teaching hospitals, and computers.   Of course, he was including in the cost of computers the commitment to systems analysis.

There is no doubt that in the future management will insist upon a better documentation of the resources required to support

all activities. Despite the pressure for a judicious allocation of scarce funds, management will continue to weigh factors
other than just dollars in its decisions. No doubt scholars in
the social and behavioral sciences can be immensely helpful
and will contribute to the development of sounder tools which
can be used to evaluate the worth of programs. Although much
emphasis is placed on dollar costs, overemphasis of dollars
alone might result in decisions which would adversely affect
society. On the basis of dollars alone — in a cost-benefit
analysis — we might price English teachers out of the market.
The same might be said of some facets of university administration.

There will undoubtedly be greater emphasis on the development
of models and associated simulation processes. This important
area of study should be encouraged, but there is the danger
that harried executives may think of models as a panacea. This
is reminiscent of the vigorous discussions which took place in
the early days of instructional television. Its strongest
adherents argued that the medium would provide a broad base
of instruction to the masses, that its potentials were unlimited,
and that through judicious use of the medium instructors could
be used more effectively. The more conservative members of
the academic community argued that at best instructional television had little, if anything, to offer. After more than
fifteen years of use and research, the value of the medium
seems to lie somewhere between the two extremes. Certainly
there are areas in which instructional television has been
most beneficial, but we have also learned that there are areas
where indeed it is of little worth. It is probable that the
same view will hold for models. This should not be construed
as opposing the implementation and use of these new tools but
rather as meant to caution eager executives not to expect too
much of them. Futhermore, while models may identify alternatives, managers will still have to make the decisions.

There will be a continued and increasing demand by agencies
outside the university for more information. As the ability
of the institutions to deliver more information improves, the
appetite for it seems to increase. No doubt the burgeoning
increases in demand for information stem partly from the fact

that the wrong questions are being asked. In an effort to derive the kind of answers which outside agencies desire, additional questions are asked and more information must be made
available. This same observation could be made in regard to
internal information requirements. In this connection there
will no doubt need to be a significant sharpening of objectives
and goals, both inside and outside an institution. More
effective guidelines need to be developed which will permit
institutions to preserve their own unique characteristics and
at the same time allow coordinating agencies to get on with
the task of providing a better perspective of the needs for
higher education within the state or region. Because of the
information which will be available to extramural agencies,
management will find it necessary to more carefully husband
and allocate its resources.

Some states are already busily engaged in the development
of information systems which, it is hoped, will not only serve
the needs of the coordinating boards but will also be appropriate to institutional management. Educational institutions
in such states, faced with the requirement to reveal all information about their operations, will be more vulnerable to
outside criticism unless their systems function properly and
provide timely information in an effective manner.

Extramural agencies will require more comparative information
which can be used as a framework for making decisions regarding
resource allocation to institutions. This requirement will pose
special problems for administrative-systems personnel since
institutional data will somehow need to be translated into
formats through which such comparisons can be made. There will
be fear on the part of many institutions that the kinds of
comparisons made from the data furnished by different schools
may not necessarily be just. This is another argument for
having an effective system that will at least put accurate information into the comparative process.

The WICHE MIS models will provide guidelines within which
institutional data can be collected and processed in useful
ways. Certainly sound comparisons should prove beneficial to
all persons concerned. It is not likely that institutions will
object to being compared where there is comparability, but the

definitions of comparability must be resolved. Unless institutional representatives face up to these tasks, someone else
will make the decisions.

Specialists in computer technology maintain that there is
no prospect of fourth-generation computers within the immediate
future. Hence, any changes which are likely to occur will
probably be executed within the existing conceptual framework.
Thus the emphasis will be on continued exploration of means by
which more information can be made available over a shorter
time span.

Research will continue in the development and implementation
of regional computer networks and their attendant software.
The change from the on-campus to the regional concept will have
a marked impact upon internal administrative systems. The
emphasis will be on standardization of administrative systems
within the region. Obviously, absolute standardization will
not be necessary, since transformations can be made of the
information which would be introduced into the network. However, translations increase the complexity of the system and
probably will be discouraged. Therefore, the alternative outcome will result in greater standardization of internal systems.
In all probability, there will be some resistance on the part
of institutions because of the fear that a standardization of
the systems will adversely affect unique characteristics which
may be peculiar to a given campus. Of course, a standard system does not necessarily imply standard decisions.

Development will continue in at least two other areas. The
first is that of parallel processing networks. Within the
existing conceptual framework, computer technologists are
developing hardware consisting of a series of computers set in
parallel which will allow bits of data to be distributed across
selective computers, calculated in parts, and subsequently
summed into components so that the speed of computation can be
substantially increased. These changes will probably not have
a great deal of impact on administrative systems per se but
will have marked significance for operating systems and the
means by which data bases are compiled.

A second technological contribution deals with teleprocessing. Although the technique is new in most universities,

the research conducted thus far appears to hold great promise.
Executives look to the day when they may have a console in
their own offices which will yield the desired computer-
generated information. A technological change of this kind
surely holds significance for administrative-systems personnel,
since the requirements will be more complex. Consider just the
matter of security of information. Decisions regarding the
location of terminals and the kinds of information which should
be made available at all levels of management will need to be
carefully reviewed.

As the capability of remote access is realized, there will
be increasing pressures upon campus decision makers to relin-
quish greater amounts of information to higher levels of
authority, and the question of who is managing the institution
will need to be evaluated. Yet those who evaluate the decisions
should have access to as much information as is available to
those who made them.

Administrative-systems-analysis techniques will not accel-
erate the need for institutional planning and long-range decision
making, nor will they speed the day when even more internal and
external information is required. Those needs and their attendant information requirements are already upon us. The new
analysis techniques will simply make the evaluation and decision-
making tasks less difficult and more likely to be effective.

[Comment by the editors. *One problem that is mentioned frequently concerning the utilization of well-developed data systems centers on the cliché, "He who controls my information,
controls my mind." The element of truth in this statement has
long been recognized by political leaders who have attempted to
increase their power through the management of information. It
is obvious that there is much potential for bias in the decision-making process, either by making information available on
a selective basis or by presenting fallacious data. The ease
with which this type of deception can be accomplished is accel-
erated as the system becomes more complex and the administrator
becomes more remote from the sources of data. Certainly much
of the decision data used in our larger universities could be
modified to an extent that would affect the outcome of a*

*rational decision process with little likelihood of the deci-
sion being discovered. This is an additional argument for the
separation of the functions of the management analyst and the
administrative decision maker. It also underscores the desirability of structuring information systems in a manner that
will facilitate validation of the data derived from the systems.
A single-entry system of financial accounting is considered to
be poor business practice. Is it not an equally poor management practice to have a single-entry system of deriving decision
data for management purposes? Perhaps information systems need
to be structured with the same type of "auditrail" verification
capabilities as are built into financial accounting systems.
This would make it possible for an outside agency (reporting
to the governing board in much the same fashion as financial
audits) to conduct periodic audits for the purpose of determining the validity of decision data. Such a procedure would
increase the credibility of decision data and reduce the sense
of malaise, felt by some administrators and members of governing boards, concerning data generated by computer-based management information systems.]*

Part II. National and regional systems.

The major impetus for the development of computer-based management information systems comes from the need to efficiently discharge complex responsibilities. The formalization and large investment of economic and human resources necessary in the development of computer-based management information systems has tended to centralize their development primarily in large, complex institutions with significant financial resources — i.e., institutions in which the variety of data and the complexities of the decision-making process make it impossible to have efficient management with traditional methods, or institutions in which the cost of questionable management practice is clearly too high.

Management information systems are funded by institutions to serve their unique management needs. The primary concern is that the system should have internal coherence with the philosophy, function, and needs of the institution which it serves. In private industry, the board of directors funds a system to serve the needs of the corporation. The system is responsible for bringing to the board information appropriate to the efficient management of the corporation. Internal coherence is the primary need to be served, and increased profits or improved competitive position are the criteria. In university management information systems, as in industry, the major function is to serve the sponsoring institution. However, the similarity between industry and education does not extend beyond this. Education is either publicly financed or, at the very least, of vital public concern. Therefore, data about the university is required outside the governing board of the institution. No simple criterion (such as profit) exists, and the analysis of the educational function requires a long concatenation of information. Further, because the board of regents is not the singular source of funding or decision making, deference must be paid to a variety of other publics — alumni, taxpayers, state education agencies, legislators, foundations, and the federal government. Thus, data collected from various institutions must be consistent and be aggregated

*across institutions as an index to what is being accomplished
and as a starting point in determining what areas of resource
allocation need special attention. This collection serves as
a basic pool of information about regional or national education. As a result, data systems which have a primary responsibility to their own institution (i.e., for internal coherence)
must also concern themselves with the generations of data that
are comparable and capable of being aggregated with equivalent
data from other institutions. In short, the political-economic
context in which the university functions demands concern with
external integration.*

*In order to cope with the problems of external integration,
regional and national agencies have been established. In the
area of academic standards, such an agency as the North Central
Association of Colleges and Secondary Schools illustrates the
drive for external integration. For management decision information, the Higher Education General Information Survey and
the Western Interstate Commission for Higher Education (WICHE)
are illustrative. The tasks such systems face are unusually
difficult because (1) the amount of data to be collected and
synthesized is great, (2) the problems of unique definition
of data elements make comparison difficult, and (3) the primary
function of the systems which feed the regional and national
center is to serve internal management needs. Fortunately,
significant efforts are being made toward the resolution of
these problems. The chapters in this Part II describe two
approaches that are being undertaken and highlight the issues
in the development of such systems.*

Chapter five. HEGIS: a report on status and plans. *Theodore Drews and Sheila Drews*

The Higher Education General Information Survey (HEGIS) is achieving a quiet revolution. Born of a conglomerate of revolutions, it has in turn spawned a revolution of its own.

Historical perspective and theoretical base

Before 1966-67 the Office of Education sent out general information forms throughout the year, seeking information on a number of subjects: students and their characteristics, the faculty, financial operations, other institutional characteristics, projections, and a variety of special inquiries. The HEGIS program sought to supersede this scattered approach and to combine all inquiries in a single package that would go out once each year to institutions of higher education. The old procedure of sending out many separate queries was in some respects easier: collection centers and responding institutions were free to concentrate on one of the surveys at a time. However, the institution often did not have its records arranged in a way to enable it to respond to the Office of Education in the format or in terms of the data categories of the questionnaire. Some institutions simply did not have the manpower available to permit them to do an adequate job.

HEGIS is a practical attempt to remedy many of these weaknesses. Under the HEGIS program, the package of forms goes to institutions early in the year — before the beginning of their fiscal year in order to give them advance notice of all that is to be asked of them in the coming year. This dating permits institutions to plan the in file and record-keeping systems in such a way that data can be easily retrieved. It also permits them to know in advance the amount of data-processing resources that will be needed to get at the data. Moreover, it permits them to schedule their work at a constant level, without peaks and valleys of activity, since the deadlines for the return of the parts of the questionnaire package are staggered.

HEGIS is also intended to help solve another problem that
troubles institutions of higher education. The HEGIS package
is intended to gather, at one time, all the general information
statistics needed by the Office of Education and other federal
agencies involved in educational programs. This process will
be described and illustrated later.

Why HEGIS was needed

In the Office of Education there is an increasing awareness
of a whole series of interrelated revolutions which are having
a profound impact on data-acquisition programs. The managerial
revolution, which has almost run its course in business and
government and brought into being the new Establishment of the
Managers, is only now coming to the institutions of higher
education. Since it has been so long delayed and is now so
imperatively necessary, it is proceeding at a forced draft.
The Office of Education is moving to meet the challenge of this
revolution — the challenge of providing management data appropriate to the decision making processes and data-collection
responsibilities of the Office of Education.

Closely related to the revolutions (which seemed to some
educators to be more convulsions than revolutions, even before
the intensification of student expressions of dissatisfaction)
within the colleges and universities are revolutionary forces
external to, but bearing heavily on the pattern of higher education. States are reaching out, with a most profound impact,
to coordinate and control the pattern of higher education within their boundaries. (This is influenced, in no small measure,
by the new federal programs.) Since the educational operations
within states are not confined to their borders, in terms of
either the influences acting on them or the influences they
exert, each of these state developments has an effect on every
other part of higher education, with a cumulative impact that
is enormous. Local governments, too, are having an effect, as
they become more active in the establishment and operation of
local institutions, particularly in the exploding junior-college
movement. In a sense, this is also a managerial revolution —
state and local governments are seeking to exert an increasing

influence in the management of programs of higher education
in order to provide as much postsecondary training as their
resources will permit. The role and participation of the
Office of Education in these activities must be maximized if
it is to meet its responsibilities of informing educational
policy and decision makers.

Finally, within this conglomerate of revolutions is the
revolution in the Office of Education itself. This revolution
is unlike the usual revolution, in that it was devised at the
top and its principles have had to be communicated down the
hierarchy, step by step. As in all revolutions, there have
been excesses. Old verities have been reexamined and discarded,
sometimes prematurely, if they could not justify their existence
immediately in highly practical terms. No apology need be made
for this. This process of swinging the pendulum too far is a
universal component of all successful revolutions. It is
essential to examine all the traditions if a distinction is to
be made between the true verities and the shibboleths.

The process of reestablishing all that was good in the
"good old days" (but those "good old days" will never return)
is under way. The Office is blending old and new practices:
combining the contributions of the solid traditionalists with
those of the imaginative innovators. In this it is building
a far more utilitarian program of statistics acquisition, management interpretation, and dissemination than has ever existed
before. There is a clear set of purposes and every acitivity
or project must meet two tests. First, it must contribute to
the achievement of those purposes. Second, it must contribute
to those purposes at a lower cost than does any available
alternative. While the phrase is much overworked and rarely
understood, this is parallel to the cost-benefit analysis of
the Department of Defense.

The role of HEGIS

The Office of Education is attempting to stay in the con-
fluence of the mainstreams of all revolutions and our discussion
will be tied to the role that HEGIS plays in this effort, and
will try to relate to this base point in proceeding beyond the

direct benefits of HEGIS to a description of some ancillary
benefits.

The National Center for Educational Statistics (NCES) is
the agency that carries out the original mandate of the Office
of Education to provide statistics on the status of education.
In functional terms the Office of Education may be described
as a national staff agency that gathers management data on the
basis of which policy makers and managers, both inside and outside the federal government, can make decisions for the most
efficient and productive allocation of the very scarce resources
available to higher education. Some specific examples of the
use of data for this purpose will be provided later.

It takes only a cursory review of the trends in higher education to realize that society is not going to have sufficient
resources available to provide all of the higher education that
will be demanded of it. Other social needs have gained increased recognition and are competing for these available
resources. (The Medicare program is prime example.) Therefore,
it is essential that a maximum effort be made to assure that
every unit of resources is allocated to do the most toward
achieving or meeting the complex demands of the society. Higher
education is distinctive from elementary-secondary education
with respect to how and where it acquires the resources that it
expends. Public elementary and secondary education is supported,
for the most part, by governmental appropriations — local, state,
and federal. Only rarely is there a contribution from some other
source. On the other hand, the support of higher education is
derived from a variety of sources. It comes from the federal
government, state governments, city governments, special dis-
tricts, student fees, foundation grants, private philanthropy,
endowments, investment earnings, bequests, and other sources
too numerous to mention here.

Current status of coordination among institutions

Except for the initial steps in some of our larger states,
there is little coordination or even intercommunication among
the institutions of higher education. In large part, they
operate as approximately 2,500 independent laws unto themselves.

Beyond the fact that no machinery exists for coordinating the operations of these many institutions, there is lack of information on the basis of which they might voluntarily coordinate their activities. Thus, institutions of higher education embark upon very expensive Ph.D. programs that produce persons trained in a specialty for which there is no social demand; they compete for graduate students in many disciplines and offer uneconomic stipends as inducements to those students; they fail to offer programs which teach young people specialties that are in tremendous demand; and they have administrators, with no administrative training and possessed of no guiding information, making decisions for the expenditure of millions of dollars which result in less than the expected maximum benefit to the educational process.

In view of today's population mobility, such that students from one coast attend college at a school on the opposite coast and graduates from one coast find employment on the other, higher education must be treated as a single operation with a total product for utilization in the whole society. It is essential not only that each federal dollar expended on higher education should achieve the maximum in benefit and utility, but also that all other dollars going to higher education should be similarly expended. Any dollar that goes down the rathole must be replaced by a dollar doing the job it could have done had it been more wisely expended. The Office of Education is the only agency possessing a sufficiently detached and objective view of the entire educational process to permit it to present data and analyses that will be accorded the respect and assumption of validity that are necessary if the data and analyses are to be used for management decisions.

The Office of Education offers information

The Office of Education does not see itself as having the assignment of telling American society what the colleges and universities should be teaching. This is a question beyond the proper realm and purview of statistics and other quantitative data. However, the Office can inform American society as to what *is* and how to accomplish any of the various ends the

society might seek to achieve. Perhaps some very simple
illustrations will make this clearer. The Office would not
presume to tell Congress, the Bureau of Higher Education, or
the general public whether it is better to produce engineers
or persons skilled in art appreciation. However, the Office
can inform them of the numbers of engineers being graduated
each year, the number that industry says that it needs, and
the cost of meeting industry's expressed need for engineers
in various cost terms, such as dollars, faculty, and other
institutional resources. The Office can make the same kind
of quantitative analysis of the supply, demand, and resource
cost of art-appreciation teachers. It may be that the educational process could produce five art appreciators for the
cost of one engineer. Policy makers at all levels, from the
federal government to a junior-college department chairman,
must make the conglomerate of decisions that will result in a
division of our educational resources among the production of
engineers, art-appreciation teachers, and all other types of
educational products. Thus, although the Office does not tell
the institutions of higher education that they ought to be
training engineers rather than teachers of art appreciation,
it does provide the Bureau of Higher Education, the National
Science Foundation, National Institutes of Health, and Congress
both directly and indirectly with the information that permits
and helps them decide, recommend, assist, and provide the
colleges with information that will help them to do either job
with a minimum expenditure of resources. Or, to put it more
generally, the Office can help them all to make informed decisions which will produce the maximum number of educated persons
in the most needed fields and within the limits of their resources. For the most part, the amount of resources does not
vary with the job to be done but in response to a multitude of
factors, not all of them related to educational need or productivity.

How HEGIS helps institutions

One of the very important side effects of the HEGIS project
has been the development of consistency in data definitions.

From the first, the entire HEGIS package has grown in consistency within itself. That is, a student, faculty member, student credit-hour, or any other term in the world of higher education is defined no differently in one part of the package, e.g., finance, than in some other part of the package, e.g., students. Also, data are being broken down, categorized, and coded identically in all parts of the package. By the end of the calendar year 1969, the National Center expects to have "A Taxonomy of Academic Disciplines" ready for application in the total HEGIS package. This is to be used wherever the data must be categorized by discipline, whether the data are on student enrollment, student majors, field for advanced degrees, fields of earned degrees, the training or assignment of faculty, the expenditure of teaching or research funds, the allocation of physical plant space, or any other subject. The data will be consistently classified on the basis of the same categories. Thus, data will be available that are consistent, compatible, and comparable. This consistency will obtain not only within the Office of Education and its publications but also among institutions.

Many state agencies (at this point they number twenty-three, but may well go to more than thirty by 1970) are joining in the HEGIS project. The result is that these state agencies are keeping their statistical records on the basis of Office of Education data categories and definitions. Thus, states may examine their own internal education problems and situations in terms that will be immediately understood on the national level. The eventual goal, which likely will not be achieved in our lifetime, is to survey the fifty state higher-education agencies. Increasingly, states are becoming involved in the survey process, which is proving to be beneficial to them and the Office of Education

One of the larger benefits of this cooperation with state agencies is that in each of these states a separate survey program has been eliminated, and to that extent the burden of preparing responses has been lightened for institutions. Thus, in at least eighteen states, a single survey sets up a data system within the institution which provides identical data for the state higher-education agency and the federal agencies.

How HEGIS helps other federal agencies

As stated at the outset, one of the early goals was to provide general information statistics to other federal agencies in order to eliminate or at least minimize duplication among the federal data-acquisition programs. This objective is beginning to be met. However, while the aim is eventually to produce publications so quickly that data may be current enough for day-to-day planning of programs, this is not always possible at the present time. In some cases, data in less finished form are all that can be provided to federal agencies. As soon as the tabulations come out of the computer and are thoroughly checked for quality and accuracy, they are duplicated and sent to the Office of Program Evaluation, Bureau of Higher Education, National Science Foundation, National Institutes of Health, and many other places. Some specific examples will demonstrate this function.

The former Assistant Secretary of HEW for Planning and Evaluation, Dr. Alice Rivlin, worked with a committee in the summer of 1968 to develop a strategy for federal support of higher education. Major reliance in the development of the report was placed on the financial and other data collected from institutions of higher education in the Higher Education General Information Survey.

The National Science Foundation receives all enrollment and degree data as well as the data on financial operations, gathered in HEGIS, in the form of a duplicate computer print-out, as soon as produced. The interest of the Foundation is primarily in the area of postbaccalaureate enrollments and degrees in the scientific fields. However, to put this data in context, information is needed on undergraduate and graduate enrollments in the nonscientific fields and on the financial operations of institutions. The National Science Foundation has been designated as the principal federal agency in the area of science education. The planning officer of NSF is actually a presidential advisor in the area of science education and provides information for planning to the National Sciences Advisory Board, the Office of Science and Technology, and the

Presidential Science Advisory Committee. In a recent presentation prepared for the Congress, the data in 30 out of 40 tables were derived in whole or in part from HEGIS.

In addition to the NSF needs for policy development data, there is an operational need that HEGIS fulfills. Some of the National Science Foundation programs require that, in order to be eligible to participate in the program, an institution must have produced a certain number of degrees in a specific field over a three-year period. Individual requests to the National Science Foundation for research support are evaluated in terms of the total financial and operational situation in the institution. This evaluation is based on HEGIS data.

In past months, the National Institutes of Health, in urgent need of data for a congressional presentation on medical facilities available in the institutions of higher education, sent members of its staff to the Center to acquire those data directly from our questionnaires. This kind of service provides data to federal agencies as rapidly as they could acquire it through their own efforts and overcomes the necessity for separate and duplicative surveys.

The Bureau of the Census, in its survey of the financial operations of state institutions, routinely uses the HEGIS survey responses to complete its data totals.

The Department of Housing and Urban Development, in the early days of its establishment, required data on the need and supply of housing on college campuses. These data are essential for the development of a rational program in a significant area of its mission. The data needs were incorporated in the HEGIS package on short notice. In this case, not only was the need for a separate survey eliminated but a new agency avoided the travail of developing a survey. This enabled the department to turn its attention to more substantive matters while the data were acquired in a routine manner.

The Congress, too, utilizes HEGIS data in a variety of ways — ranging from telephoned requests for particular data items to the provision of detailed special runs out of the computer. In the last Congress, for instance, the Senate Subcommittee on Education requested enrollment data on two-year colleges. These were provided from our data file on the enrollment in all

institutions, and the statistics were printed as a special
subcommittee document.

Within the Office of Education, the HEGIS data are the
primary source of statistical support when the commissioner
makes his presentation to the Congress. Many of the programs
now in being (such as the Higher Education Facilities Act, the
Higher Education Act, the National Defense Education Act, the
Adult Education Act, and the Vocational Educational Act) were
developed and justified on the basis of statistical data provided by the National Center or (prior to its establishment on
January 1, 1965) by the Division of Educational Statistics.
The Office of Program Planning and Evaluation within the Office
of Education uses these survey data to evaluate the success of
the programs with a view to making recommendations for their
modification.

In a description of the HEGIS data and its impact on and
utility for the formulation of federal policies, at least
passing mention should be made of the role of the various
associations of higher-education institutions. Frequently
these associations are invited to testify before congressional
committees and to advise policy makers in the executive branch.
A significant portion of the data on which they rely for the
formulation of their recommendations is derived from the
National Center.

Developmental perspectives

Now, to look ahead to the future. As a general view, if
the data acquisition system can be routinized, if much of the
burden on the respondents can be eliminated, and if consistency
can be achieved in the data banks of institutions, state
agencies, other federal agencies, semipublic educational
associations, and the Office of Education, then attention
can be directed to an even more important task. This is the
more intimate involvement of the Higher Education Studies
Branch in the development of information needed for the formulation of federal policies and in the evaluation of the impact
of federal programs and activities. Although this branch has

no responsibility for the direct development of policies or evaluations, the higher-education specialists who are intimately involved with all phases of the acquisition, management and dissemination of data can provide technical assistance to those who do have these responsibilities. Extensive and intensive interpretation of these data, as to the meaning and implications of the statistical relationships that they display, has not yet been provided to the policy makers. The Higher Education Studies Branch will not be playing its most useful role until this potential is realized.

There is also a potential role in the analysis of data for assistance to institutions of higher education on the operations level. The growing function of institutional research in institutions of higher education, which is often just another way of saying "operations research," has tremendous needs for data which will serve as a guide in more effective utilization of resources.

Survey activity, which seeks information from the institutions themselves, will not, under present plans, change greatly during the next decade. Of course, it must be borne in mind that there are two major determinants over which the Office of Education has no control and which are predictable in a limited sense only. The first of these is the type and quantity of statistical data that will be required by the Congress, the executive departments, and the higher-education community. The second, which may be more influential and less predictable, is the quantity of resources that will be available. The most urgent needs and the most thoughtful plans mean little in the face of a lack of funds and staff. Thus, the following discussion is conditional on the two assumptions that the types of demands for data will not vary significantly from what is anticipated and that staff and resources will be available.

It is planned to begin acquiring data on admissions standards at the institutions beginning in February 1971. This is probably one of the most important questions in the prospective student's mind and a question which must be studied in connection with the broadening of opportunities.

Standardizing codes

Related to the work with institutions (but not directly involved in the Higher Education General Information Survey) is the active participation of the Higher Education Survey Branch in the work of a subcommittee of the Federal Inter-agency Committee on Education. That subcommittee is charged with the responsibility for defining, categorizing, and codifying the postsecondary universe of data. A part of this task has already been completed, and uniform codes of institutions of higher education are now contained routinely in the *Higher Education Directory*. During February 1970 it is planned that uniform abbreviations will be developed for the names of institutions and for academic fields, both for computer input and publications output. In the coming years this subcommittee plans to work on the development of uniform component designations and their appropriate categorization and coding.

Plans for student data

In the area of student data, there is a long history of more than twenty years in which data of certain kinds are collected and published annually. Among these are gross enrollment totals, some enrollment detail, enrollment for advanced degrees, degrees and other formal awards granted. Such collection and publication will continue throughout the next decade without substantial modifications except for improving and reorganizing the arrays of academic fields, making various breaks of the data as needs are communicated to the Center, and the like.

The study of the residence and migration of college students was begun in the fall of 1958 and was repeated in the fall of 1963 and the fall of 1968. Tentatively, it is planned that the study will be repeated in the fall of 1973 and the fall of 1978. However, the 1968 results will be reviewed to determine whether the quinquennial period offers sufficient frequency for adequate analysis of trends in the migration of students from state to state. If the trends suggest that the study needs to be made

with greater frequency, present plans will be subject to change.
This is an extremely important and sensitive area of data,
since the support of public institutions impinges on taxpayers
of a particular political jurisdiction. There is understandable
apprehension with respect to the numbers of students coming
from outside the boundaries of that political subdivision to
participate in the educational program.

In the Higher Education General Information Survey, conducted in the fall of 1967, an attempt was made to acquire
data on all enrollment in the upper division of the undergraduate level (replacing the earlier Biennial Survey of enrollment by field in the junior year). It would be well if
resources would permit this to be repeated biennially so that
manpower agencies could anticipate the number of graduates in
the next few years.

With increasing pressure on institutions of higher education
to make year-round use of their facilities and staffs, the
numbers of students enrolled in the summer is increasing. In
the light of this trend, the amount of activity in the summer
period is being measured. In the fall of 1966 and the fall of
1967, HEGIS acquired data on both students and faculty for the
summer period. These data are being analyzed and will provide
guidance for the continuation of activity in this area during
the next decade.

The federal agencies which would like to support increased
activity in particular fields, as well as those which are concerned with manpower output and the amounts of training given
in particular fields (even though this training may not result
in a degree), are interested in numbers of course enrollments.
This has always been an exceedingly difficult concept, and
there is not yet agreement as to how such surveys should be
conducted. By fiscal year 1972 (in the fall of 1971 – HEGIS VI)
it is hoped that the capability of conducting a pretest of a
procedure to acquire course enrollments in selected fields will
be present. With what would be learned on this pretest, an
annual survey of course enrollments could be conducted. Data
could be acquired in various fields in different years, thereby
establishing trend data for the fields having the highest
degree of interest.

The key to measuring the workload of the faculty, faculty
productivity, and the unit cost of instruction is the acquisition of data on student credit hours taught by disciplines.
If plans and priorities permit, such a survey could be pretested in fiscal year 1971, acquiring data for the preceding
academic year, 1969-70. Based on this pretest, the survey
probably would have to be operated for three succeeding con-
secutive years until the trendlines were firmly established.
Thereafter, the survey could be conducted on a biennial basis.

Prospects for data on costs

One of the major questions asked by all those who would
provide support to students in higher education is How much
does it cost the student? There are large amounts of data on
this subject, but there is great disagreement as to what kinds
of costs to the students should be included. The National
Center has reviewed a number of plans to conduct a pretest of
a sample survey of students to discover the costs of such surveys. Such plans could be ready by fiscal year 1971 for a
pretest based on academic year 1970-71. Based on what would
be learned in such a pretest, the survey could then be conducted at some appropriate interval beginning in fiscal year
1972.

Manual planned

Beyond the activities in the area of students, HEGIS is
presently participating in the development of the previously
mentioned manual on academic fields of specialization. This
is being done in cooperation with the Western Interstate
Commission on Higher Education. Once complete, and accepted,
this manual would be used for the listing, categorization,
definition, coding, and aggregation of academic fields and
areas of specialization for all statistical areas that require
such a break. These areas include students, faculty, facilities,
finance, degrees, etc.

Later history of students

An important question which has had relatively little investigation is that of the degree to which college training
actually fits the graduate for whatever vocational activity
he undertakes. The National Center's highest education
specialists would like to undertake a sample survey of college
graduates and follow them for a few years after they have received their degrees and entered upon their chosen employment.
Such a survey could be pretested in February 1972, with the
major part of the survey in February 1973. Thereafter, the
chosen group could be followed up for three years to determine
whether their employment is closely related to the work they
undertook in college and the degree to which a proportion of
them followed some other endeavor. The development of such a
survey program would be entirely dependent on resource availability and priorities.

Prospects for data on faculty

In spite of the fact that the numbers, type, and condition
of the faculty (particularly in the light of the growing need
for faculty) have been areas of tremendous interest, the
Center's data collection in this field has not been adequate.
Therefore, in the Fall of 1968 a new and experimental survey,
on a sample basis, sought to acquire data on the faculty by
fine field. This study is currently being processed and
analyzed. Hopefully, it may provide a major input to the
understanding of academic fields. In addition, it will provide, for the first time, national totals for faculty in institutions of higher education broken down by particular fields.

In HEGIS IV, for the year 1969-70, the faculty survey effort
is being kept to a minimum. The Center will acquire only data
on faculty salaries by rank.

In HEGIS V, 1970-71, it is hoped that resources will permit
a major effort in the area of faculty, so that data might be
acquired with respect to the numbers of faculty and other staff
by function and by fine field (derived from the academic fields

manual), the number of summer faculty, the degrees held by the
faculty, the background and the experience of faculty, faculty
retention by institution, and faculty teaching loads (a sample
pretest). In the succeeding year, 1971-72, data could then be
gathered on faculty salaries by discipline, and in addition
there could be a survey on faculty teaching load based on the
preceding year's pretest. Thereafter, the numbers of faculty
by function, and fine fields, probably ought to be gathered
annually. Data on numbers of summer faculty probably need not
be gathered more often than quadrennially. Data on faculty
salaries would be most useful if gathered as a major effort
biennially, with a minor effort to gather summary data in the
years between. Data on degrees held should be gathered quadrennially, as should other information on the background and
experience of the faculty. Accompanying this should be the
quadrennial survey on faculty retention. Again, it must be
emphasized that the major determinants will be priorities and
resource availability.

As regards teaching loads, the sample pretest could take
place in 1970-71, if funds become available, with the full
survey in 1971-72. Following a year in which the data are
digested, the survey would be repeated in 1973-74. It is likely
that another repetition would not be required until 1977-78.

In the Fall of 1972 there should be a pretest on the research
activity of the faculty. Depending on the availability of funds
and the success of that pretest, a full survey would be run in
the Fall of 1973 and in the Fall of 1977.

In non-HEGIS acitivity, during the fiscal year 1970, resources
permitting, it is hoped that a survey of a sample of faculty
can be undertaken to discover faculty motivation in accepting
employment in various kinds of institutions. The purpose of
the survey would be to discover what it is that makes a faculty
member accept employment at one institution rather than another.
The study would seek to identify and analyze the importance of
various characteristics of institutions and incentives in
attracting staff members. This survey would be followed up two
years later, during 1971-72, to trace what happened to the
faculty in the original sample.

Plans are being reviewed to develop during the year 1970-71 a manual of faculty data and definitions. This manual would assist the federal government, the states, and the institutions in achieving greater consistency in faculty data.

Prospects for data on finances

There is as much (or more) interest in the area of higher education finance as in any other data area. While there may be interest in students, faculty, and other kinds of statistical data, it is the questions of the dollars available that determines whether or not an institution will operate and the level on which it will operate.

Beginning in the Fall of 1966, the National Center acquired, annually, data on current revenues and current expenditures. Hopefully, this will be continued throughout the next decade. These are the only finance data that are being gathered in HEGIS IV. Beginning with HEGIS V, which goes out in the fall of 1970, throught is being given to the biennial gathering of data on capital receipts as well as information on capital loans, physical plant debt, and endowment.

Data on physical-plant fixed assets were originally planned in HEGIS IV, but a lack of processing resources required their elimination. There is hope that these data will be gathered in HEGIS V and biennially thereafter. Information on student financial aid could be gathered in HEGIS V and VI, and thereafter biennially.

The annual gathering of information on federal funds ought to be scheduled to begin with HEGIS V.

Unit-cost data or activity-cost data in institutions of higher education have not been collected heretofore and will not be included sooner than HEGIS V. If this collection is successful, and if resources are available, a full survey, taking up both research operations and unit costs, could be conducted in the Fall of 1971 and the fall of 1973. The survey of research operations costs could then be repeated in the Fall of 1975; the unit-cost survey could be repeated in the Fall of 1978.

It is important to discover the sources of support for higher education and to discover and analyze the present and prospective capacity of those sources. As is well known, higher education receives its financial support from a variety of agencies both public and private. If the federal government is to make meaningful plans relative to support of higher education, it will need to know the capacity of the present sources of support. This is beyond the scope of HEGIS, but the Center has been studying this question, during the past year, through a contract with the American Institutes for Research. That work is not yet completed. A survey should be designed during 1969-70, based on the background now being developed. This survey could be presented during 1970-71, and the full survey could take place in 1971-72.

The development of a manual of definitions and procedures on financial statistics is planned. The American Council on Education has a manual of accounting categories and procedures. However, accounting records are not adequate for statistical analyses. Data must be put into formats that are usable by statisticians. The Center's manual would attempt, while maintaining consistency with the accounting records, to categorize and define financial statistical data in a manner that makes it more appropriate and more usable for statistical analyses.

Data on buildings

For a number of years the federal government has had programs which provide facilities for higher education. During the initial years of these programs, allocations of funds to institutions for construction of a facility were in response to desperate needs. However, future programs for higher education facilities must be based on information, such as the amount and type of facilities that currently exist and the manner and effectiveness of their use.

In cooperation with a committee of the Executive Directors of the State Higher Education Facilities Commissions, the Center developed a manual for inventorying physical facilities in 1967. The Higher Education General Information Survey carried a facilities questionnaire based on this manual in the Fall of 1968. This first effort asked for data on the type of space, its function, and some limited information on the academic field.

HEGIS IV, which is a minimum package, asks for information only on type of space and function. In response to users' requests, consideration is being given to an annual inventory of type and space. This might be omitted in the Fall of 1972 when the total burden on respondents with respect to space would be great.

Inventorying by function is taking place in the Fall of 1969. Hopefully, resources will be available to repeat it in 1970. Thereafter, a triennial survey seems to be appropriate. Beginning in the Fall of 1970, the inventory by academic field could also be carried on as a triennial survey, if priorities permit.

Many users have made known their need for both data and standards on the condition of space. The earliest date at which an experimental survey could be conducted would be Fall 1971. Institutions of higher education would be asked for information on the condition of their physical facilities and about the revision of categories and definitions. Thereafter, the survey might be conducted biennially.

In the Fall of 1970, a minimal pretest of the utilization of instructional space in institutions is desired. This would be followed by a full survey on the subject in the Fall of 1971 and 1972. If the priorities and resources permit this, minimal data could be acquired in the Fall of 1975 to discover whether conditions have changed sufficiently to merit a total study. Assuming that they have not, the next full-scale study of the utilization of instructional space would not need to take place until the Fall of 1978.

In the Fall of 1971, it is hoped that resources will be available for running a pretest of a survey to measure the utilization of research space, public service space, and administration and service space. Based on this pretest, a full-scale survey of the utilization of this kind of space could be developed in the Fall of 1972. If all went well, there might then be a minimum survey in the Fall of 1975 to discover whether conditions have changed. This could be followed by a full-scale study in the Fall of 1978 (unless the Fall, 1975, survey indicated that this would need to be done sooner.).

The surveys on space utilization will be made possible by virtue of a manual on measurement of space utilization which is

currently being prepared by the Space Utilization Committee of
the Association of Executive Directors of the Higher Education
Facilities of the Bureau of Higher Education. It is anticipated
that this manual will be nearly complete during 1969-70 and
published during 1970-71. With this publication the Center
would be able to enter upon a program of measurement of space
utilization, and with substantial funding, logical programs of
higher education facilities would be possible for the Congress.

HEGIS as a vehicle of management information

In conclusion, it should be emphasized that HEGIS, which began primarily as a device to make a procedure more efficient,
has been the focus of a really revolutionary acceleration in
the development of a national system of management information.
It may be that HEGIS merely appeared at the right time to be
used as such a vehicle. Certainly it is true that HEGIS merely
appeared at the right time to be used as such a vehicle. Certainly it is true that HEGIS does not yet cover all the areas
of data that will eventually be needed by researchers, policy
makers, and managers. However, HEGIS includes an ever-increasing
core of data (scheduled for major expansion in the coming decade). Moreover, HEGIS is developing a national system of data
acquisition that is compatible and consistent among federal
government agencies, national associations of institutions and
educational specialists, regional associations of institutions
and state agencies, state higher education agencies, educational
researchers, and the institutions themselves. While there is
clear understanding that the data needs of each of these groups
vary, particularly with respect to the amount of detail that
they require, there is no doubt as to the value and the essenti-
ality of compatibility, or at least convertibility, of all their
data files.

[Comment by the editors. *The financial inputs from the
federal government to higher education are significant in the
present and are likely to be even more so in the future. Therefore, the potential impact of the Higher Education General Information Survey on the colleges and universities is difficult*

*to overestimate. Because of this the thoughtful and provocative
critique of the Drews' paper, as presented by George W. Baughman,
is included here in its entirety.*]

Critique by George W. Baughman

The issue of a new direction for the National Center of
Educational Statistics is a most critical one for the higher-
education community. Changing the image and capabilities of
the Center from that of being the source of opening fall enrollment counts, degrees awarded, occasional national projections
of educational statistics, and some statewide educational
statistics and the repository of vast amounts of unused data to
that of being "a national staff agency that gathers management
data, on the basis of which policy makers and managers, both inside and outside the federal government, can make decisions for
the most efficient and productive allocation of the very scarce
resources available to higher education" requires a number of
heroic assumptions.

If the goals of NCES are to serve management, then the paper
should clearly state what is meant by management (e.g., Health,
Education and Welfare, National Science Foundation, State Boards
of Higher Education, Regional Coordinating or Accreditation
Agencies, individual institutions), and the existing and proposed
studies should indicate how they serve the planning, organizing,
and control functions of the "management(s)" served. For
example, what management group(s) and function(s) are served by
opening fall enrollments? Are these data viewed as social
indicators designed to reflect progress in terms of national
and/or statewide and/or institutional objectives (evaluative
control)? Are they the basis of forecasting trends (planning)?
If so, for whom? Are they intended to be matched with theoretical capacities to indicate where resources are available
(organizing)? Or are they collected and published as general
information that may or may not be interesting to any management
 group.

Further, if management information rather than general information about universities is the goal of N.C.E.S., then it

must be able to communicate with the management(s) it intends
to serve. It must be aware of and sensitive to objectives,
goals, organizational structures, operating procedures, data
needs, and soon, of management. This is most unrealistic at
the institutional or state level. It is highly questionable at
the federal level. In short, it seems far more realistic for
N.C.E.S. to focus on providing general information that is
frequently referred to on a timely basis rather than to attempt
to become a "management" information center.

In fact, this horizon is most evident in the current collect-
ions of data, in the twenty-four additional proposed surveys,
and in the recent survey of "Needs for Educational Statistics."
This document is particularly naive if viewed from a management
standpoint (e.g., item 6. Do you now use or have you used
educational statistics in the last two years?) but would provide
a beginning tally of general information interests.

By dropping the management notion, one can apply the author's
mandate of having a "clear set of purposes and every activity
or project must meet the test of being contributive to the
achievement of these purposes and of providing more of that
contribution to those purposes at a lower cost in our resources
than does any available alternative." Surveys of interests
of possible users of data are most appropriate to a general-
information activity. Purposes then can be defined in terms
of specific user groups served without attempting to evaluate
the management value to the user. Existing and proposed studies
can be evaluated and perhaps funded on the basis of user demand.

In the context of general information for a variety of users
at lowest relative cost there are still serious theoretical and
practical flaws in the current Higher Education General Information Survey (HEGIS) approach to information collection and
dissemination. These flaws become magnified in the large number
of proposed surveys and should be rectified. The suggested
additions to the HEGIS package could produce increasingly complex
and expensive measurements of highly suspect derived "standardized" elements, aggregated into extremely dubious "comparative"
cells, with a strong probability of being burdensome to many
and useful to few.

APPENDIX   A

DEPARTMENT OF HEALTH, EDUCATION, AND WELFARE
OFFICE OF EDUCATION
WASHINGTON, D. C. 20202

NEEDS FOR EDUCATIONAL STATISTICS

BUDGET BUREAU NO. 51-S69001
APPROVAL EXPIRES: 3/31/69

1 2 3 4

1. NAME (LAST, FIRST, MIDDLE INITIAL)(TYPE OR PRINT) | 5 6 7 2. TITLE

8 3. SPECIFY YOUR MAJOR FUNCTION RELATING TO EDUCATION (CHECK ONE)

☐¹ PLANNING (CURRICULUM, FACILITIES, PROGRAMS, ETC)   ☐⁵ MANAGEMENT

☐² RESEARCH   ☐⁶ COMMUNICATIONS MEDIA

☐³ ADVISORY   ☐⁷ OTHER (DESCRIBE)

☐⁴ MARKETING

4A. NAME OF ORGANIZATION | B. ADDRESS

5. TYPE OF ORGANIZATION (CHECK ALL APPLICABLE BOXES)

9 ☐¹ PUBLIC EDUCATION   11 ☐ GOVERNMENT AGENCY   12 ☐¹ PRIVATE INDUSTRY

☐² PRIVATE EDUCATION   ☐¹ FEDERAL   ☐² OTHER (DESCRIBE)

10 ☐¹ ELEMENTARY OR SECONDARY   ☐² STATE

☐² HIGHER EDUCATION   ☐³ CITY/COUNTY

13 6. DO YOU NOW USE OR HAVE YOU USED EDUCATIONAL STATISTICS IN THE LAST TWO YEARS?
☐ ☐¹ YES   ☐² NO

14-37 7. IF YOU ANSWERED "YES," INDICATE THE TYPE(S) OF EDUCATIONAL STATISTICS YOU HAVE USED. (CHECK THOSE WHICH YOU HAVE USED, ACCORDING TO THE APPROPRIATE LEVEL OF EDUCATION.

TYPE OF EDUCATIONAL STATISTICS	ELEMENTARY AND SECONDARY EDUCATION	HIGHER EDUCATION	OTHER
STUDENT INFORMATION	14	15	16
STAFF INFORMATION	17	18	19
FINANCIAL	20	21	22
FACILITIES AND EQUIPMENT	23	24	25
CURRICULUM AND INSTRUCTION	26	27	28
EDUCATIONAL LEVEL ATTAINED	29	30	31
INSTITUTIONAL CHARACTERISTICS	32	33	34
COMMUNITY CHARACTERISTICS	35	36	37

38 OTHER (EXPLAIN BRIEFLY AND INDICATE LEVEL OF EDUCATION
☐

39 40 IF YOU ANSWERED QUESTION 7, GO BACK AND PLACE A CIRCLE AROUND THE ONE
☐ ☐ CHECK WHICH BEST INDICATES THE KIND OF STATISTICS WHICH IS MOST IMPORTANT TO YOU.

OE FORM 2311-1, 1/69

8. WILL YOU HAVE A NEED FOR EDUCATIONAL STATISTICS DURING THE NEXT TWO YEARS?

☐ 1 YES   ☐ 2 NO

9. IF YOU ANSWERED "YES" TO QUESTION 8, INDICATE THE TYPES OF EDUCATIONAL STATISTICS YOU WILL NEED DURING THE NEXT TWO YEARS. (PLACE A CHECK OPPOSITE THOSE YOU WILL NEED, IN THE APPROPRIATE COLUMN REFLECTING LEVEL OF EDUCATION)

TYPE OF EDUCATIONAL STATISTICS	ELEMENTARY AND SECONDARY EDUCATION	HIGHER EDUCATION	OTHER
STUDENT INFORMATION	42	43	44
STAFF INFORMATION	45	46	47
FINANCIAL	48	49	50
FACILITIES AND EQUIPMENT	51	52	53
CURRICULUM AND INSTRUCTION	54	55	56
EDUCATIONAL LEVEL ATTAINED	57	58	59
INSTITUTIONAL CHARACTERISTICS	60	61	62
COMMUNITY CHARACTERISTICS	63	64	65

OTHER (EXPLAIN BRIEFLY AND INDICATE LEVEL OF EDUCATION)

☐ 66

IF YOU ANSWERED QUESTION 9, GO BACK AND PLACE A CIRCLE AROUND THE ONE CHECK WHICH BEST INDICATES THE KIND OF STATISTICS WHICH WILL BE THE MOST IMPORTANT TO YOU

☐ 67 68

10. DO YOU NEED EDUCATIONAL STATISTICS WHICH ARE CURRENTLY NOT AVAILABLE TO YOU?

☐ 1 YES   ☐ 2 NO

11. IF YOU ANSWERED "YES" TO QUESTION 10, PLEASE DESCRIBE BRIEFLY THOSE EDUCATIONAL STATISTICS YOU ARE UNABLE TO OBTAIN.

☐☐ 70 71

12. LIST TWO OR THREE INDIVIDUALS IN YOUR ORGANIZATION WHO MAKE THE MOST SIGNIFICANT USE OF EDUCATIONAL STATISTICS. IF NONE, WRITE "NONE."

NAME	TITLE	DIVISION, BRANCH, DEPARTMENT, ETC.

13. COMMENTS

Consider the following propositions:

A. The communicative value of statistical information-is dependent upon six factors: (1) the population included, (2) the reporting horizon, (3) the nature of the measurement, (4) the definition of elements, (5) the level of aggregation, and (6) the timeliness of receipt.

B. The absolute cost of collecting statistical information increases directly with the size of the population, the frequency of collection, the distance of the reporting horizon (forward or backward) from a current time period, the complexity of the measurements derived, the degree of sophistication and standardization of elements collected, and the level of desired comparability in aggregations.

C. The relevance of complex measures, standardized elements, and comparative aggregations is dependent upon simple measures, transactional elements, and intrainstitutional aggregations.

D. Increasing the number of bona-fide users of general information will reduce the relative cost of the information and is dependent upon increasing the communicative value and relevance of measures, elements, and aggregations.

A brief analysis of current HEGIS surveys indicates that they are primarily interested in measuring single-set inventories (e.g., enrollments, type of space); using standardized elements (e.g., a full-time head count being equal to a student taking 75 percent or more of a full-time load); aggregated into inter-institutional generic categories (e.g., "Senior Staff") and organizational categories (e.g., Social Sciences are ———).

There is little knowledge in the surveys regarding multiple-set measures (e.g., Do the student data relate to finances or space?) and little about the transactional elements that form the basis for the standardized elements or about the intra-university generic or organizational classifications used in developing "comparative data," and this lack presents serious weaknesses. For example, how many institutions actually carry a separate "standard" identifier of full-time, based on a criterion of 75 percent of full load, in their student trans-actional data? Further, if we suspect that the "standard" is not expressible in transactional units, of what value is it? Certainly the British Thermal Unit (B.T.U.) would be meaningless if one could not define 1 Fahrenheit-degree changes in 1 pound of water. Aggregated and derived statistics based on uncertain standard elements usually display more symmetry than sense.

If we pretend to understand or have comparability when each institution is assumed to be able to make generic and organizational translations of its data without the benefit of seeing how any other institution has made similar decisions, we are treading on statistical quicksand. Increasing the number of translations by expanding the generic and organizational categories only enables us to be more precisely wrong. Recent systems developments in Indiana and Colorado have gone a long way towards revolving these problems by requesting data to reflect both intrainstitutional and interinstitutional modes. Numerous efforts are being made to collect transactional elements that will enable the sound development of standard definitions for interuniversity comparisons.

There is some evidence of this concern (and of its value) in the HEGIS efforts to provide pretests on questionnaires. However, the results of such efforts frequently demonstrate the versatility of universities in making sense out of nonsense or vice versa rather than actually addressing the validity of the exercise. For example, the 1968 sampling of full- and part-time faculty by major field of teaching and research required the following:

a. Development of standardized data elements based on a persons total activity (e.g., full-time or part-time) and then assigning that element to a predominant generic (senior or junior staff) and activity (instuction, and departmental research) and organizational unit.

b. Providing "comparative" generic aggregations based on title and/or rank as well as on funding, again dependent upon the predominant test.

c. Providing "comparative" organizational aggregations (academic fields) based on institutional departmental affiliations or subgroupings or departmental affiliations.

In our case a rather elaborate generalized computer program determined the elements and aggregates required, using decision tables that included title code, object-of-expense, fund-group,

and academic-department code mappings, along with some detailed
logic, to determine the predominance of an activity. Although
the final product does in fact balance to total transactional
input, there are only three persons in the university who can
interpret what is really in the cells. Further, since the report does not in any way reflect actual organizational affini-
ties, it is not particularly useful for exchange purposes.

In short, that particular report cost the university about
$2,000 to prepare and provided no internal benefits. On the
other hand, if the report were reflective of transactional
elements and intrauniversity generic and organizational aggregations, as well as our attempts to provide "comparative
translations", it could be a most valuable one to the university.
Not only could it be used to show internal management what
categorizations of our people are currently used or ignored for
federal purposes, but it could also serve as a valuable interuniversity exchange document. In the latter case, those who
used the "comparative" or standard data could actually see what
institutional criteria were used.

My fears are that the plethora of new studies suggested by
N.C.E.S. will only add to the recent trend to develop "standard"
data elements that are complex deviations from transactional
elements and aggregations that reflect minute categories out of
context with the institutional setting. These fears are further
highlighted by the type of measurements suggested in the proposed
studies. The majority of the proposed studies involve surveys
of activities (e.g., enrollments in courses, student credit
hours taught) and complex inventories (e.g., faculty by field
and function), whereas current surveys have generally been
simple inventories (e.g., opening fall enrollment, migration,
and residence). A tabulation of current and proposed surveys
appears in Table 1. The elemental data used in this "standardized," aggregated, statistical summary appears in Table 2.

To the casual reader, Table 1, like most of the published
HEGIS reports, appears to be a straightforward statistical
summary. That is, it is symmetrical; it appears to be comprehensive; it utilizes what appear to be standard definitions
and comparable aggregations. However, for anyone who wants to
work with or question the taxonomy, Table 2 reveals the actual

surveys covered, as well as the aggregations and elements used in arriving at the statistical summary. Without this background the data in Table 1 are not useful to the analytical evaluater. Comparisons of the tabulation in Table 1 with others drawn using the same "definitions" would be as meaningless as building bridges between sand bars if the bases were not made evident.

Table 1. *Analysis of current and proposed U.S.O.E. surveys by type of survey and timing of survey*

Type of survey	Current					Proposed				
	Ann.	*Bian.*	*Quin.*	*Other*	*Total*	*Ann.*	*Bian.*	*Quin.*	*Other*	*Total*
Student inventory	3	1	1		5				1	1
Student activity	1			—	1	1	1		2	4
total	4	1	1		6	1	1		3	5
Faculty inventory	1			1	2	1	1	3		5
Faculty activity		—	—	1	0				3	3
total	1			1	2	1	1	3	3	8
Financial inventory									1	1
Financial activity	1	—	—	—	1	1	1		2	4
total	1				1	1	1		3	5
Space inventory	1				1	1	1		2	4
Space activity		—	—	—		2				2
total	1				1	3	1		2	6
Total inventory	5	1	1	1	8	2	2	3	4	11
Total activity	2				2	4	2		7	13
grand total	7	1	1	1	10	6	4	3	11	24

Today's technology does permit, and today's real information needs do require, closed-loop and complete communications. These can now be accomplished rather easily. For example, if elemental data are necessary for a standardized definition, collect the elemental data and the standardization method. If organizational aggregations are desired on a comparative basis, collect the data in terms of intrainstitution coding and indicate the "standard code" as well. This relatively simple convention will permit real two-way communication between the institutions and the users of standardized, aggregated data. It will enable "central" editors to determine if comparability does hold by seeing how the various institutions interpreted the "standards" and aggregated their own units. Further, it will make possible a simplified data-collection system, in that requests for data and data reports can be tailored to the institution's structure by sorting on the institution's code sets.

Table 2. *Listing of current and proposed HEGIS projects*

	type 1*	timing 2*
A. *Students*		
1. *Current bases*		
a. Opening fall enrollments - gross totals	I	A
b. Degrees granted - by academic field	A	A
c. Enrollment for advanced degrees by field	I/A	A
d. Migration and residence (1968)	I	Q
e. Upper division undergraduate (1967) by field	I	B
f. Summer enrollments	I	A
g. Definition of student terms		
2. *Proposed changes and additions*		
a. Course enrollments in selected fields (1971p, 1972)	A	A
b. Student credit hours taught by field (1970p, 1971)	A	B
c. Cost to student (1970p, 1971)	A	?
d. Common codes for all academic areas		
e. College graduates, progress after degree (p1972, 1973)	A	4 yr.
f. Admissions standards (1970)	I	?
B. *Faculty*		
1. *Current*		
a. Faculty by FT, PT. by academic field	I	?
b. Faculty salaries by rank (1969-70)	I	A
2. *Proposed*		
a. Faculty and other staff by function by academic field (1970)	I	A
b. Number of summer faculty (1970)	I	Q
c. Degrees held, background and experience (1970)	I	Q
d. Faculty teaching loads (1970p, 1973, 1977)	A	?
e. Faculty salaries by rank and academic field	I	B
f. Research activity of faculty (1972p, 1973, 1977)	A	?
g. Manual of faculty data and definition (1970)		
h. Faculty motivation for employment (1969, 1971)	A	?
i. Faculty retention (1970)	I	Q
C. *Finance*		
1. *Current*		
a. Total current revenue and expense by source, fund and function	A	A
2. *Proposed*		
a. Capital receipts, capital loans, physical plant debt, and endowments (1970)	A	B
b. Federal funds information (1970)	A	A
c. Unit cost or activity cost (1970, 1971, 1973)	A	?
d. Research operations cost (1971, 1973, 1975, 1978)	A	?
e. Study of sources for support (1970, 1971)	I	?
f. Manual of definition for financial statistics		?
D. *Space*		
1. *Current*		
a. Space inventory manual		
b. Type of space, function, academic field (1968)	I	A
2. *Proposed*		
a. Hegis IV - type of space and function (1969)	I	?
b. Annual space inventory (1970, 1971, 1973)	I	A
c. Inventory by function (1969, 1970)	I	A
d. Inventory by function and academic field (1970)	I	T
e. Condition of space (1971)	I	B
f. Utilization of instructional space (p1970, 1971, 1972, 1975)	A	A
g. Utilization of research space, public service space, administrative and service space (p1971, 1972, 1975)	A	A
h. Manual on space utilization		

*1 type code   A-Activity report related to instructional research or public services processes
I-Inventory report on the amount of units or dollars of input or output or resource factors available e.g. personnel, space, financial

*2 timing code   A-Annual
B-Biennial
T-Triennial
Q-Quinquennially
?-Uncertain other than as specified by dates

The ultimate of this approach would be to have N.C.E.S.
maintain statistical data sets and "dictionaries" of terms on
a rather modest computer (e.g., 256K) with large, medium-speed
storage media (e.g., data cells) and teleprocessing capabilities.
The data sets would be maintained in both institutional and
standard modes, and institutions could tag individual data sets
as to confidentiality. Since access times could be considered
in terms of hours or days rather than minutes, inexpensive
terminals and communications networks could readily be utilized.
In this setting an institution with a large number of external
requests for data could in fact utilize this service to fulfill
requests by suggesting subsets of either the institutional or
standardized codes. To go one step further, "questionnaires"
could be phrased (by reference to the dictionary of available
data) by institutional or standard terms and sent via mail or
teletype to the sample population. If the institutions surveyed
okayed the specific release, then the National Center could fill
the request via terminal or mail. This would reduce considerably
the plethora of data survey (e.g., Ohio State processed over 150
separate requests for salary averages in 1969, frequently using
specific subsets of departments). It would provide considerable
information to those designing surveys about the institutions
that were to be surveyed, their organizational structures, natural data structures, etc., as well as having ready access to
"prestandardized" and aggregated data.

For the first time, institutions, as well as state, regional,
and national organizations or agencies, could spend their
energies on analysis instead of on designing surveys and tabulating inconceivable data. This, in fact, would provide the
vehicle for accomplishing the revolution that is needed in the
national data-collection effort.

Chapter six. The Western Interstate Commission for Higher Education Management Information Systems Program. *Ben Lawrence*

The need for the MIS Program

The rapid growth in size and complexity of higher education has highlighted the need for systematic collection and use of data in the management of colleges, universities, and state systems of higher education. On the one hand, the college administrator is faced with an array of difficult decisions as he contemplates the rising costs of maintaining existing programs, the increasing numbers of students to be served, the necessity of improving quality, and the demands for new and expanded services. On the other hand, he faces the reluctance of the taxpayer to provide the necessary resources, by increasing the tax burden, without a significant justification for the increasing costs. In justifying rising budgets and deciding where to allocate scarce resources, the administrator should be able to calculate the costs of various alternative courses of action and relate them to some measurement of achievement of institutional objectives.

Without systematic, accurate feedback to the administrator concerning the effect of its operations, an institution or system can waste its resources on ineffective and unnecessarily costly activities. Judgments aobut effectiveness and relative costs, however, cannot be made adequately in isolation. Institutions need comparable data from other institutions of similar complexity and with similar missions as a basis for evaluating the efficiency and effectiveness of their own internal operations. State coordinating agencies need comparable data from institutions under their jurisdiction in order to make wise choices in the allocation of resources among institutions. The federal government needs comparable data in order to allocate resources wisely among competing educational programs and to evaluate effectively the provision of educational services to the nation.

Recognizing the need for improved information retrieval, analysis, and reporting, representatives from state coordinating agencies and concerned colleges and universities in the West asked the Western Interstate Commission of Higher Education (WICHE) to undertake a program designed to facilitate the development of managment information systems within institutions of higher education. More specifically, they called for the development and implementation of compatible data bases including standard data elements and standard procedures, formulas, and models, in order to facilitate the exchange of comparable information among institutions of higher education and, further, to improve reporting to the state and federal levels. This request has resulted in the devlopment of the WICHE Management Information Systems (MIS) Program. This program proposes to encourage the development of management information systems within higher education institutions which will be sufficiently individualized to serve the unique needs of the respective institutions and at the same time be sufficiently compatible to allow valid interinstitutional data comparisons, as well as promote efficient reporting to state and federal government.

The Board of Higher Education in Illinois and the State University of New York were requested and have agreed to participate in this program. This enlargement of the participation base arose out of the desire to have other institutions of the size and complexity of those from the state of California involved in the program. These substantial additions to the thirteen western states, coupled with the federal funding of the core program staff, bring national significance to this regional program.

The diversity in size, type, and quality of the institutions participating in this program requires coordination, compromise, and cooperation. This was the basis on which the program was conceptualized and the funding proposal was developed. This is also the continued policy for implementation — a small capable staff coordinating the cooperative efforts of the participating institutions and agencies. Both the proposal design and Phase I efforts have been concerned with the delineation of objectives and assumptions underlying the program.

Objectives of the MIS Program

The overall objective of this program is to develop management information systems designed to improve decision making
for resource allocation in higher education within the institution, at the state level, and at the national level.

The delineation of the broad overall objective has proved
to be somewhat more difficult than might be imagined. The
initial choice of the words "management information systems"
has created semantic problems that are difficult to surmount.
The relationships among different types of information systems —
"total information systems", transactional information systems",
"electronic data processing systems" — and the widely varying
definitions applied to these terms have made it difficult to
delineate the objectives of the program and to communicate
agreements reached by the design and steering groups to the
participating institutions.

The overall objective of this program — the development of
management information systems designed to improve decision
making for resource allocation — requires analysis and data.

Institutions of higher education are nonprofit, service-
type agencies. Administrators cannot look to the profit-and-
loss statement to determine the efficiency of their institution
in relation to other institutions. These are not dependent
upon the acid test of the marketplace as a source of their
operating funds. The relationship between revenue and expenditure is at least tenuous, because revenue comes only in small
part through the consumer, that is, the student.

In the absence of this handy aggregate indicator of
efficiency — profit — service agencies must undertake serious
analysis of their operations in the light of specific, well-
defined objectives. The WICHE MIS Program envisages the
development of analytical models, related to the problems faced
by decision makers, as the most appropriate analytical technique
now available. Through the use of analytical models, alternative
courses of action may be identified that will produce specified
objectives. At the same time, the relative costs of the alternative courses of action can be determined.

Data are required in order to carry out this analysis and to operate the models. Consequently, the WICHE MIS Program is concerned with identifying and defining the data elements needed to operate the analytical models devised.

In the very narrow sense, the WICHE MIS Program consists of the development of analytical models pertaining to resource allocation and the identification and definition of the data elements necessary to operate the models. However, since the necessary data elements are best obtained whenever possible through "transactional information systems," such as the "payroll system," the "registration system," or the "accounting system," and because comparability of information is important (as will be explained later), the program must give some attention to the problems of collection, storage, retrieval, and analysis of data in data systems in order to make them usable in the models. While the program proposes to make suggestions in this important area, the problem of collection, storage, and retrieval of data is considered to be the task of the institution and not central to the MIS Program (see Figure 1).

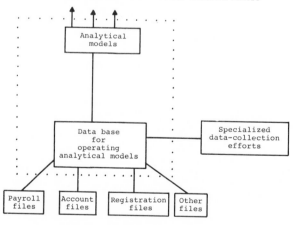

Alternative courses of action for decision makers

Analytical models

Data base for operating analytical models

Specialized data-collection efforts

Payroll files

Account files

Registration files

Other files

The dotted line encloses the primary area of concern for the WICHE MIS Program. Relationships with transactional information systems are important but secondary.

Figure 1.

Constraints

Early in the development of the program, at least four constraints were identified as necessary to the operation of the
program. The first necessary constraint is that the management
information systems that are developed must be adaptable —
adaptable not in the sense that they can handle anything, but in
the sense that they can be modified without rebuilding the entire system. This constraint is necessary for two reasons. In
the first place, the state of the art in the development of
information systems is changing so rapidly that many changes
may be anticipated in the course of the next year or two. The
systems that are developed must be able to adapt to these new
technologies and new demands. In the second place, the management information system cannot be developed at the expense of
the successful operation of the transactional systems within
the institutions. These transactional systems — the payroll
system, the registration system, the accounting system — must
be viable units within themselves. They must have the option
to change when it is necessary to meet their own needs in reporting and transactional outputs. Systems might be designed
in the way a submarine is designed. A submarine is a highly
integrated operating unit, but it contains many compartments
that can be sealed off in an emergency while it maintains its
basic seaworthiness. Information systems are needed that are
highly integrated but sufficiently compartmentalized that basic
changes can be made to a particular part of the system without
jeopardizing the integrity of all of the systems. For example,
the various operating systems — the student information system,
the accounting system, the payroll system — must be able to
stand alone as operating units, but they should also be capable
of being interrelated so as to form a common pool of basic data
for the serving of a management information system. Given
adequate planning resources, it is now possible to design systems
with these characteristics.

The second necessary constraint is the development of a
clear explication of the goals and objectives of the institution
or process the management information system is being designed

to serve. The risk of responding to crisis demands for information with "quick and dirty surveys" can no longer be run.
Systems designed to respond to questions within the context of
overall goals and objectives must be developed. With this more
precise definition given to goals, the problems become more
apparent. Models can be built that will describe the system,
and information needs will move from the infinite to the finite.
Instead of gathering all feasible information, only information
which is necessary for the understanding of the most pressing
problems will be required. This approach has two very practical
advantages. (1) It reduces considerably the amount of information theoretically required — a practical consideration in view
of the costs of storage and retrieval of information, and (2)
it assists in reducing the quantity and complexity of information before it is generated rather than after it is generated.

The third necessary constraint is that information systems
must be developed that apply as few restrictions as possible —
preferably none — on the operation and development of the
respective, unique institutions of higher education. While
some restrictions will and must be placed upon institutions,
they should not be placed there by the information system but
as a result of the management decisions that are made on the
basis of information that accurately describes the institution.

One of the major strengths of higher education in America
is the diversity of the institutions providing the services.
This is to be encouraged, and management information systems
should permit this deversity.

The fourth important constraint is that management systems
must be developed that *simultaneously* provide information for
    1. Management within the institution,
    2. Interinstitutional comparison and study, and
    3. Reporting at the state and national levels.
This requires compatible management information systems.[1]
Management information systems are compatible either when they
are identical in every respect or when they can otherwise produce comparable pieces of information.

Identical management information systems do violence to the
third constraint applied to the development of the systems and
are therefore rejected. How can management information systems

be developed that can otherwise produce comparable pieces of
information in order to meet our definition of compatibility?
Commencing with the assumption that institutions of higher
education have common problems, it follows that common analytical models can be developed that will assist in the solution
of those problems. If the problems that are most pressing
among a significant number of institutions can be agreed upon,
the resources necessary to develop such analytical models can
be gathered.

Each model chosen for operation requires a finite list of
data elements for its operation. This finite list of data
elements may be termed a "data base." If compatible information
systems are to be developed, common or standard data bases must
be adopted. If a data base is to be common or to be standard
among institutions of higher education, each element must be
defined in precisely the same way, and the respective bases of
each institution must contain all of the necessary elements.

The collection of data bases for the respective models may
be called "the standard data base." Given such a standard data
base, an institution may produce information that is unique to
the institution and required only for its internal operation.
It would do this through the aggregation of specific data
elements according to its own prescribed model or its own
prescribed formula. It could, for example, develop its own
unique student full-time equivalency using a formula such as
$\frac{A + B}{C}$, where A, B, and C are individual data elements in the
standard data base. On the other hand, it could develop information that is standard for comparison purposes with other
institutions, such as a standard student full-time equivalency,
perhaps being composed from the elements A, D, and C according
to the formula $\frac{A + D}{C}$. This assumes that the respective basic
data elements A, B, C, and D in each of the respective bases
are defined in precisely the same way.

There are, of course, other factors that affect the degree
of compatibility among management information systems. At this
point the question must be asked: How compatible should these
systems be? Other factors affecting the degree of compatibility
among management information systems are codes, field formats,
file structures, software programs, and hardware. These terms

all pertain to technical matters of storage, retrieval, and analysis of data by computer process.

However, as compatibility is increased by adopting standard codes, field formats, file structures, software programs, and hardware, the systems become more nearly identical. This tends to apply more constraints upon the institutions than is desirable.

It may be useful to develop suggested codes, field formats, file structures, and perhaps even software programs for institutions that have not yet developed their own management information systems to any degree in order to have a ready-made system available for adoption or as a guide for the development of their system. However, it does not appear advisable at this time to try to bring about compatibility by developing standardization beyond the concept of a common data base and the development of common analytical models which would be used for management information exchange.

Given a standard data base which might include a set of standard data elements, a set of optional standard data elements (that is, data elements that may not be required for the operation of all analytical models but for which a standard definition is recommended), and a set of data elements that is unique to the institution's needs, it is possible for the institution, through its own unique data structure, codes, field formats, and file structures, driving its own unique management models, to develop unique information for management within the institution. On the other hand, using that same standard data base kept according to the institution's own unique data structure — it is possible by means of interface programs, conversion programs, or transformation programs (whichever is the most appropriate term) to restructure the data elements in a form suitable for operating common analytical models or management information exchange models, in order to produce information that is comparable with that produced by other institutions using that same standard data base.

Program activities

Phase I of the WICHE Management Information Systems Program has been completed and Phase II is beginning.[2] The analytical

task force of the WICHE MIS Program has specified a priority
list of activities under Phase II to be undertaken by the WICHE
MIS staff and the institutions. Some of these activities will
be undertaken simultaneously, and in fact some of these activities are already well under way. The list is not designed to
provide a sequence of events, but rather to insure that the
staff and institutions are on a goal-oriented path. These
activities are detailed below.

*1. A public explication of college and university conceptual
models.* As was indicated earlier, if analysis is to contribute
to better decision making on resource allocation, colleges and
universities must know and understand their objectives. The
WICHE MIS Program has the task of developing a conceptual model
of the colleges and universities which, in effect, specifies
very general objectives. For the time being, the analytical
task force has concluded that there are three major programs
in our college and university systems today — instruction, research, and public service. And these have three supporting
elements — libraries, administration, and various support
services. As a part of the WICHE MIS training program, several
possible conceptual views of colleges and universities will be
explained and a rationale for the adoption of one view for
purposes of information exchange will be developed.

2. The development of compatible data bases. These data
bases will include standard data elements — that is, data
elements defined in precisely the same way. The data bases
will also identify optional data elements — data elements that
may not be necessary in the immediate future for the exchange
of information among institutions or reporting to the state and
federal levels but which, if an institution chooses to include
the element in its data base, should be kept according to a
standard definition. In addition, the data bases will include
unique data elements — elements that are unique to the institution.

This activity will lead to the production of a standard data-
element dictionary which will define the data elements and
classify them according to specified uses. For example, it will

indicate which data elements are typically used by the institution, which will be required for responding to the Higher
Education General Information Survey, and which will be required
for participating at various levels of participation in the
WICHE MIS Program. Should funds become available, it is proposed
to develop suggested codes, field formats, and file structures
for use in collection, storage, retrieval, and analysis of the
data within the data system. If this activity is undertaken,
a supplement to the standard data-element dictionary will be
issued setting out these suggested standard codes, field formats,
and file structures.

*3. The development of procedures for obtaining and exchanging
costs of instruction by level of student and field of study.*
This will be done, basically, through the development and implementation of a program classification structure together with
the supporting analytical studies necessary for producing the
cost information desired.

In order to classify transactions uniformly and produce
comparable cost information, a manual will be necessary to
provide consistent definitions of the major programs (instruction, research, and public service), to list typical subprograms
and program element classifications, and to define a set of
information categories to be attached to each program element
of the program classification structure.

The information categories necessary are these.

1. Cost categories — personnel, plant maintenance, supplies,
   etc. A model crossover computer program will have to
   developed to permit routine and periodic crossover of
   transactions from the regular accounting structure.
2. Physical resources assigned — equipment, facilities,
   personnel.
3. Indicators of activity — enrollments, student credit hours,
   number of research projects, etc.
4. Indicators of output — e.g., successful program completers
   as indicated by degrees earned and certificates awarded.

It will also be necessary to develop analytical models to
relate the data in the various information categories mentioned

above to produce costs of instruction per student by level and discipline and estimated throughput rates or productivity rates, which together will yield cost per unit of output in the instructional area.

4. *The conceptualization and development of analytical models designed to use the information generated through the program classification structure and its information categories to predict the consequences of various courses of action.* These will include initially

1. A resource requirements prediction model having the following outputs:
   (a) Specification of required physical resources — (1) personnel, including both academic (by type and discipline) and nonacademic, and (2) physical facilities by type and discipline;
   (b) Full specification of capital and operating costs, as categorized by the program classification structure;
   (c) Unit instructional costs at desired levels of comprehensiveness for students at each level in each discipline.

2. A student flow model having the following outputs:
   (a) The probability of achieving a particular goal given certain student and institutional characteristics;
   (b) Variations in goal achievement probability given changes in input.

5. *To begin the development of procedures or techniques for determination of the relationship between costs and benefits of the instructional functions.* Cost-benefit analysis is not just around the corner. However, it is time that this technique be applied to the process of higher education in an exploratory way. This will require the determination of the quality of the student on admission to the institution and on completion of the program. If this is possible, then hopefully the difference between the quality of the student on admission to the program and the quality upon completion of the program, which might be referred to as "value added," can be determined. Relating value added to the inputs in the instructional function will yield a theoretical cost-benefit relationship.

Immediate results are by no means assured. This task is being undertaken with a great deal of skepticism, but at the same time it recognizably has enough merit (particularly in view of waning resources and increasing demands) to warrant thorough study.

6. To develop and encourage the development of training programs, both short- and long-term, in the use and development of management information systems. The need to provide training programs and to encourage the development of training programs for users and developers of management information systems is apparent. There is a considerable communication gap between users and developers of management information systems. Training is necessary if this gap is to be closed. Users need to have a better understanding of the techniques and possibilities in the development of management information systems if they are to be expected to support the development of sophisticated management information systems which, at present, are costly.

The extreme shortage of persons appropriately trained in the techniques of analytical study and persons trained in the development of sophisticated data systems is even more apparent. It is not proposed to undertake a massive technical training program directly. However, it is proposed to encourage the development of such programs in institutions of higher education in the participating states and to use these institutions, in cooperation with the WICHE MIS staff, in the development of short-term seminars designed specifically to meet the needs of the long-term development of management information systems.

The WICHE MIS Program proposes to undertake its activities initially in the area pertaining to the instructional function. As time permits, it will undertake to implement management information systems in the areas of research and external service. However, it is more important to concentrate on one area to begin with, and the most important area appears to be the instructional function.

The Management Information Systems Program of the Western Interstate Commission for Higher Education is now well under way. Phase I has been completed, and the bulk of the staff has been recruited. The Program includes the major institutions of higher education in the thirteen western states, New York, and Illinois. The central staff is funded by the U.S. Office of Education under a five-year continuing contract. While the staff is employed by the Western Interstate Commission for Higher Education, the program is guided by a steering committee made up of representatives from the institutions and agencies within the participating states and by a National Advisory Panel made up of representatives from the various regional and national organizations having an interest in the development of management information systems.

The activities of program development are carred on through a series of task forces, two of which are presently operating. These are the Data Element Task Force and the Analytical Studies Task Force. It is envisaged that other task forces will be appointed as they are needed. The operational philosophy of the program is that the staff serves the institutions through the task forces that represent them. Accordingly, it is hoped to encourage the development of compatible management information systems within the participating institutions. This development will promote better management within the institution and at the same time provide the capacity for the exchange of information among institutions and for reporting to state and national government agencies.

The success of this program is dependent upon the continued support of institutions and agencies of higher education at both state and national levels.

[Comment by the editors. *The author of this chapter has outlined an approach for improving decision making, relative to resource allocation in higher education, through the development of analytical models. Since such models have as a fundamental prerequisite the clear statement of institutional objectives, the development of these objectives is particularly critical to the approach outlined. The extreme difficulty of specifying even general objectives in most institutions of higher education is apparent to those who have attempted the task. Assuming that institutional objectives can be clearly defined and stated, three other problems emerge. First, quantifying these objectives and developing criteria for the measurement of progress toward their realization is at best an arduous task. Second, it is difficult to identify all of the variables which may be pertinent in evaluating progress toward an objective. This is complicated by the conflict which exists between the desire to minimize the data requirements of the system and the need to search out such variables. Third, the variables selected are to be used among a variety of institutions. Therefore, the validity of the analysis requires the assumption that, in measuring movement toward the realization of any specified objective, the criterion variables and their interrelationships are functionally the same in all institutions concerned, even though they vary significantly in type, function, and size.*

In recognition of the fact that established data systems have been developed primarily to serve the internal needs of some particular institution and that a restructuring of the elements of the various data systems is not easily achieved, the WICHE MIS approach places heavy reliance upon conversion programs. Implementation of such programs is frequently found to be much more difficult than is apparent at the outset. It may be argued that, since few institutions have well-established computer-based information systems, more emphasis should be placed on the development of a recommended basic information system, one that could be adopted by institutions as each moves toward the development of its own system. If such basic information system was well designed, it could be adopted completely by many institutions. Institutions contemplating changes in their existing systems might also find it desirable to adopt many elements of the basic information system. In this way considerable impetus could be given to the development of common data systems.]

Notes

1. Ben Lawrence, *Compatible Management Information Systems: A Technical Report Concerning the Concepts Underlying Compatibility in the WICHE Management Information Systems Program*, Boulder, Colo., WICHE, 1969, pp. 1-7.
2. *Phase II Objectives and Time Schedule of the WICHE Management Information Systems Program*, Boulder, Colo., WICHE, 1969.

Part III. Modeling as a tool in management information systems.

That modern computer technology has had dramatic impact on the lives of all of us is a truism. That it has dramatically changed out management practices in our more complex institutions, both public and private, is apparent. Many types of analyses that were understood in theory but not utilized in practice, because of cumbersome problems in data gathering and analysis, are now commonly undertaken. Of these, none is more exciting or offers a higher potential than the techniques of modeling or simulation. The first paper in this section describes the concept and methodology of model building. Particular attention is paid to the state of the art in higher education. The major difficulties encountered in modeling are presented, and the use of simulation as technique for experimentation and prediction is discussed. Primary emphasis is given to the purposes and benefits associated with modeling, and a series of recommendations for developing this capability in universities and colleges is offered.

The three chapters that follow represent widely different approaches to what is essentially one and the same problem — providing a method for determining the probable outcomes of changes in the academic program structure on the space, time, and human resources of the university, and thereby providing an aid to educational planning and decision making.

Chapter seven. Modeling for higher education administration and management. *Robert A. Wallhaus*

A model is a representation of reality — abstract or physical. Modeling reality is commonplace and has long been practiced in various areas of man's endeavors. The planetarium of the astronomer, road maps, the pilot unit constructed by a chemical engineer, organizational charts — these are just a few examples of such representations.

A primary purpose of a model is to facilitate modification and experimentation of reality. It may be infeasible and uneconomical to change the real system for purposes of investigating new configurations or predicting future behavior. For example, an astronomer cannot manipulate the universe, and it would be uneconomical indeed to eliminate the curriculum in mathematics in order to observe the effect on the institution. This mode of investigation has been appropriately call "trial-and-disaster". It is often practical, however, to modify *a model* of the real system and to assume that the conclusions drawn are also valid for the real system.

In general, models depict systems characterized by elements and the interrelationships between them. The goal in modeling is to capture the attributes of the elements and the interrelationships so as to mirror the system which the model represents. This means that the model builder must describe the parameters and variables of the model as well as the relationships and the constraints on system components.

Models are classified as follows by Elmaghraby. (For this and other named references, see the select Bibliography at the end of this chapter.)

1. *Structural models,* limited to depicting the elements of the system and the interrelationships. The graphical representation of the university in Figure 2 is an example of this type of model.

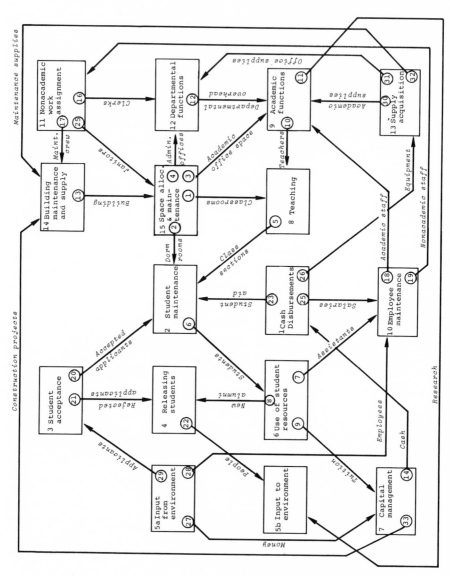

Figure 2. *Structural graph of the university*

2. *Functional models,* which describe the "flow" processes relating the elements of the system and usually give particular attention to input-output mechanisms. Most mathematical models are of this type. The relationship between space allocation and academic staff, shown as an arrow in Figure 2, might be described by the mathematical model $S_t = f(t)$, which says that office space S_t is equal to a function f of the number of academic staff t; where f is a mathematical expression. All other arcs in Figure 2 could be similarly "modeled."

3. An *iconic model* "looks like" the object it represents. An architect's model of a building (scaled down) is such a model; so is a Ping-Pong-ball model of an atom (scaled up).

4. An *analog model* substitutes one property for another. For example, a hydraulic system of pipes, valves, and reservoirs can represent cash flows.

In order to properly design a model it is necessary to identify its purpose. Models are generally utilized in one of the following ways.

1. They may permit feasible and economical experimentation on real-world systems without incurring the costs, risks, and expenditures of time which may be required in actuality.

2. They allow us to formulate, communicate, and discuss hypotheses.

3. They bring about an understanding of the system variables and their relationships.

4. They make it possible to forecast and project for planning and decision making.

5. They allow control of the time scale. Real-world processes occur over long periods of time. Modeling can allow long time intervals to be collapsed.

6. They enable us to control and monitor real-world processes.

An extremely complex system, such as higher education, dictates that we back off somewhat from the more ambitious purposes of modeling. Models of higher education can help explain issues which arise in planning the direction that an institution is to take in the future, and thereby aid in formulating educational and administrative policies. The most effective use of modeling

in education is as a tool to provide information in the form
of decision alternatives, cost estimates, and indications of
probable results.

System complexities give rise to a conflict of interests
which is inherent to some degree in all model building. On the
one hand, it is necessary to be detailed and explicit in the
description of various model components in order that they may
reflect the reality being studied. On the other hand, complexities are introduced as a function of the amount of detail,
which may detract considerably from the utility of the model.
This conflict of interest "raises its ugly head" very stren-
uously in the case of higher education.

A model will never represent dynamically changing reality
exactly because of the uncertainties which exist in describing
the real system. In fact, replication of reality is not desired, since it will obviate the reasons for modeling. It is
necessary to simplify or abstract from the real system to allow
practical formulation and testing. It is also important in the
formulation of models to allow for flexibility in the use of
the model and let the model be structured in such a way as to
facilitate manipulation and experimentation. Questions regarding the desirable degree of abstraction or simplification
can be answered only as a function of the purpose of the model
and must be weighed against the practicalities of the cost of
construction and experimentation.

Much thought and discussion have been presented elsewhere
relative to the problems encountered in modeling the educational
process. The following pages attempt to collectively document
the major difficulties.

Defining the system to be modeled.

Since a model is a representation of a set of entities and
the relationships between them it is necessary to define what
set of components is to be included in a model. Usually it is
possible to generalize a series of relationships between elements until virtually the entire world is encompassed. For
example, in modeling the institution, certainly the student is

a major element in the system.   There is, further, a relationship
between the student and his parents, which may be significant
in describing the behavior of the institutional system — depending, of course, on the purpose of the model.   This line of
reasoning can be extended to include past generations of relatives or associates.   However, such relationships are usually
considered to be relatively insignificant and are therefore
not included as model components.   Consider the structural model
in Figure 2, which assumes a specific system of elements and
relationships.   It may be argued that certain key elements are
missing or perhaps it will be judged that some elements like
"supplies acquisition" need not be included, because they show
unimportant effects on the behavior of the system.   The assumption of frictionless pulleys in mechanical systems and the
neglect of unemployment rate in inventory modeling are similar
attempts to specify only the more important elements and to relieve complexities.   Resolving the question of significance is
a key decision in defining the system to be modeled.

Gathering the data to support modeling

The model builder is faced with the need to determine values
for the model parameters and specify the behavior of the system
variables over time, as well as to define the relationships
between the components of the system and the exogenous effects
of those components not included in the defined subsystem.   The
analyst must contend with the problem of developing an information system which will supply the data necessary to specify and
maintain the model.   As expressed by Kilbridge et al.,

> models without data are sterile.   What is needed is not
> merely more data but the right data in the right form.   To
> collect or record data meaningfully requires at least a
> working hypothesis as to how it will be used: without this,
> there is no rationale for deciding what data to collect, no
> principle for ordering the data, once gathered.   To be useful,
> data must be kept over time so that it can be used for trends,
> time series, and comparisons.

The model cannot be data driven, that is, entirely influenced
by what data are available; but it is unrealistic to construct
a model and then hope that the necessary data can be obtained.

The answer to this dilemma, although not an entirely satisfactory one, is to iterate between the stages of model construction and information-system development.

Model building efforts must be tempered by the feasibility of gathering data, and the information system must be oriented to the purposes of the model with an eye to resolving incompatibilities between the model and the information system. Inconsistencies within the historical data, such as beginning-term course data used with end-of-term student data, must be avoided by obtaining snapshots, so to speak, of the institutional files at particular points in time.

In modeling the educational institution the key variables and relationships are very often subjective and difficult to include. For example, student unrest, politics in the state legislature, and the economic condition of the state or nation may be significant in describing the institution. Even if such conditions could be rigorously defined in explicit terms, specific variables are difficult to identify, and gathering data relative to these variables poses a confounding constraint on the development of a realistic model.

The question of the degree of disaggregation depends on many factors — the availability of data, the economics of data collection, the purposes of the model, the constraints on the computational requirements of the model, and the structure of the system being modeled, including the amount of stratification which is possible. In describing the student sector of Figure 2 it is necessary to answer whether class level, sex, age, etc., must be uniquely identified. Aggregation, of course, tends to cloud the details, whereas disaggregation may render the model virtually useless, due to infeasibilities in obtaining data or performing experiments.

In a university environment it is desirable to utilize operating data from such files as payroll, student records, space inventory, and personnel as a basis for the data required in the model. Maintaining such data has usually been justified for operating purposes and the data are generally available and accurate. In addition, well-defined systems for gathering and maintaining them usually exist. (At the University of Illinois a considerable amount of data is available, in machine-readable

form, in virtually every sector shown in Figure 2.) This raises
the question whether operating data are driving the model. There
is a further question whether such data are consistent and
yield a true representation of the institution. But it can be
argued that information which is required by the model represents the significant processes of the institution, and if this
is the case, it should be made available for operating and control purposes as well. The role of the information system *and*
the model is to contribute to the decision making process. Since
the model and the information system are directed toward the
same end, inconsistencies between the data base to support
modeling and the information system should be minimized in
order to maximize utility.

The first steps in model building should center on identifying output variables which contribute to planning and decision
making, policy variables over which university management has
control, and the linkages between output variables and policy
variables.

Technical difficulties in model building

While model relationships are generally easier to handle
if they can be assumed to be linear, such is not often the case
in a complex system.

Most of the variables are not continuous but rather exist as
step functions in reality. Consider, for example, the discrete
jump in net assignable square feet (NASF) of space which become
available when a new building is constructed. Such discontinu-
ities often become insignificant in the aggregate but cannot be
overlooked. The University of Illinois recently conducted a
regression study aimed at deriving a predicting equation for
NASF required by an academic department (Amundsen). A number
of different models were tried but in every instance an unacceptable discrepancy existed between actual and predicted.
This discrepancy was due, in large part, to the inherent
differences between academic departments. It could be relieved
somewhat by grouping similar departments and deriving predicting
equations for each group.

A trade-off between resources certainly exists in reality but is difficult to capture in a quantitative statement. That is, it is generally possible to trade staff for equipment, etc. However, it is often not possible to define this relationship explicitly, and the criteria function associated with such trade-offs is difficult to formulate mathematically. An analogous trade-off relationship exists between inputs and outputs; for example, research may be substituted for instruction and vice versa. This is an especially acute problem in educational systems and obviates the possibility of specifying a quantitative goal function. For these reasons the state of the art does not permit "solving a global model" in the sense of optimizing an objective function. The future state of the art does not look very promising either, as one reflects on the divergent views of the students, faculty, administration, and public relative to the goals of the institution — not to mention the means for attaining them.

The educational system is dynamic, and the key elements may change with time as do the relationships between the model components. For example a significant educational change currently gathering momentum is the trend toward interdisciplinary programs. Physicists and mathematicians are working on social problems, psychologists are contributing to engineering design in the space age, and electronic and computer scientists are developing new tools for instruction.

Must models perpetuate suboptimal use?

A common criticism of models is that they often represent a propagation of past errors into the future. Certainly institutional modeling is open to such criticism, primarily due to the common use of existing ratios between resource and input-output measures; for example, student-staff, space-staff, etc. Such ratios are based on historical utilization of resources which may have been and continue to be suboptimal. It is very likely that modeling on such a basis will yield an unrealistic projection of planning variables to attain institutional goals, especially if a more effective utilization of resources can be accomplished. There is even greater danger

that the institution will be lulled into assuming that such
ratios *cannot* be changed in the future and will continue to
operate in the suboptimal mode of the past as a way of life.
This thought was expressed by an administrative intern from
the University of Mexico after he had spent a number of months
in America studying various universities and their planning
process in particular:

> It is somewhat painful to see how human organizations, un-
> like nature's organizations (animals) "eat" (take in activ-
> ities, volumes, and resources) without limit and "grow" fat
> and sick. The organizations are unable to change and adapt
> due to their high inertia, with overloaded systems and an
> alienation on the behavior of their human members that leads
> to crisis....Of course, such monsters become famous (like
> circus phenomena do) and the natural reaction is to breed
> them even more and to keep them alive no matter what their
> true effectiveness is. I wonder why the Higher Education
> System has not strived for a well-balanced growth of its
> units. Some of them starve while others grow almost limit-
> less until the administration and the government go through
> the painful process of losing control [Flores].

Problems of model implementation

One of the first questions to answer in model building is
the question of who is going to use the model and for what
purposes. Constructing a model which embodies the capabilities
desired by the decision maker who is to use the model and then
communicating to him the limitations and assumptions must be a
primary concern of modeling in higher education. There must
be an overpopulated Boot Hill for models — some buried by users
and others by theoreticians. They all display very nearly the
same epitaph:

> Here lies an expensive tool, an expenditure of considerable
> talents — unfortunately, it solved no problem, but created
> some and had to be destroyed

and

> Here lies a valuable theory, an example of the latest tech-
> nology — unfortunately, it *had* no problem to solve, but a
> little creativity and support could have saved it.

There seems to exist some sort of no man's land between the
operational use of the model in a decision making environment
and the theoretical development of the model, which must be
bridged if a useful purpose is to be served. Bridging this gap

is a responsibility of both the theoretician who builds the
model and the decision maker who uses it; and failure is a re-
flection on both parties. If this gap is not closed, there is
a great danger of model misuse or disuse and even attendant
disaster.

The information or solutions which are derived from the model
are a function of the techniques utilized in construction and
experimentation. During the stages of model manipulation the
analyst will be building in assumptions, bringing to bear various
techniques. All of these activities may change the output of
the model, and so the essence of these functions must be
communicated to the model user. In a like manner the decision
maker must communicate the purpose for which he desires a model
and the problems which he is attempting to solve. This specification will generally take the form of an identification of the
output variables which the decision maker considers to be important. Basically the decision maker needs a description of
the uncertainties contained in the model, a description of the
structural relationships and the significance of these relationships between the input-output and functional variables, and a
description of the assumptions embodied in the model. Perhaps
some discipline could be identified to bridge the gap between
the scientist or theoretician who constructs the model and
the decision maker who implements the model — call it an engineering function. The engineer's responsibility would be to
aid in interpreting and implementing the theory of the model
in the decision maker's environment, concentrating on assuring
that the model is not misused.

Problems of model validation

Model validation is concerned with ensuring the correctness
or validity of the model and evaluating its contribution to the
purpose of which it was constructed. The key to model validation is perhaps expressed best by McKenney:

> The criteria for success is: Does the model fulfill its pur-
> pose?....The issue of "is the model true or not" may be
> dormant since the important question is: will it allow reason-
> able estimates of an anticipatory nature...? Whether a model
> has predicted or not is often a function of what the predic-
> tion is to be used for.

Proving that the model is "true" implicitly assumes that we have the means (criteria) for distinguishing between true and not true. State in another way, there must exist a yardstick which can be used to measure the results of the model in terms of a comparison with reality. This yardstick usually take the form of historical data. One of the primary techniques for validating a model is to use it in a retrospective prediction of history (use past data to describe the parameters and relationships) and assure that conformance to observable behavior exists. For example, if we utilized an enrollment mix for a given term in the past and the model indicated a need for twice as many staff as were actually required during that term, we would probably have to reject the validity of the model.

It has been claimed that models perform their predictive function well only when the future is very similar to the past. This represents a somewhat dismal situation, since deviations from historical behavior usually cause the greatest difficulties in effective planning and control. While there is little questions that the model builder often encounters this dilemma, he should recognize that not all systems are in the same state at the same point in time. Much can be learned by observing comparable systems that have previously passed through states which have not yet been experienced by the system being modeled. For example, the California system of higher education has for some time had a multi-campus university and a well-developed junior-college structure. Such a system is just now emerging in other areas of the country.

The model builder should give attention to defining lagged relationships between variables, since this facilitates accurate prediction. For example, enrollment rate may lag disposable family income level by twenty years. If a high correlation between such time series variables can be established, the means for predicting long-range enrollment rates based on existing data could be incorporated into a model. There are many examples of such lagged relationships. A good case can be made that instructional trends lag research trends, but models in higher education have not, in general, capitalized on the possibility.

A number of statistical techniques can be utilized in the model validation phase: goodness of fit measures such as chi-square tests, factor analysis, and analysis of variance are useful but usually at a micro level. Sensitivity analyses can be particularly useful in verification and determining which elements of the system to include in the model. Of course, there is an economic limit to how far such statistical testing can go, and usually this limit is set considerably short of complete validation.

In summary, validation attempts to prove that the model is a reasonably true representation of reality within the context of its purpose. While a number of techniques for accomplishing this verification have been identified and are described in more detail elsewhere, the state of the art is something less than satisfying.

Simulation

What techniques are available for using or "solving" the model? In some instances, by the time a valid model has been obtained, it has already served its most useful purpose — namely, furthered an understanding of the real system. However, there are techniques which can be utilized to fulfill the purposes for modeling identified above. It is beyond the scope of this paper to treat in detail even a representative portion of these problem-solving methodologies. Instead the following remarks concentrate on one such tool — simulation — which will undoubtedly play a significant role in higher education modeling.

Simulation is not a theory, nor is it a solution technique in the usual sense; rather it is a methodology for experimentation and prediction. The word "simulate," which *Webster's Collegiate Dictionary* has defined as "to assume the appearance of, without the reality," implies the essence of the technique. Having captured the appearance of reality in a model we want to "run" the model through time. Usually, it is not interesting from a problem-solving standpoint to view the system at an instant in time; rather, it is necessary to observe the behavior of the system over time. Simulation, then, increments time in terms of the variables and relationships of the system. In this way the simulation plays out the scenario which is representative of reality. The decision maker can thus watch a replica of reality "pass by" and utilize what is learned as a basis for actual decisions.

The valuable power in simulation is attained when various decisions or system states are tested by modifying the parameters or relationships and resimulating. Such modifications may be classified as either parametric or functional. Parametric simulations change the value(s) of certain model elements. For example, it may be desirable to investigate the behavior of the university system under a different set of student-staff ratios. Functional simulations (or a simulation on rules) modify the relationships between model elements. As an example, consider changing the "class sectioning" relationship between the Teaching and Student Maintenance sectors of Figure 2 to be handled directly by the Space Allocation sector — perhaps using a different mathematical function to describe this new relationship.

While it is confounding to perform a large number of perturbations simultaneously (there is usually the problem of explaining the cause-effect relationship), it is obvious that many different configurations can be run by slightly changing the model. The decision maker can investigate alternatives in a what-if fashion, and the model can be utilized to predict possible outcomes as a function of various inputs.

In most cases the model incorporates certain stochastic elements. Capital input from the environment in Figure 2 may vary considerably from year to year. The simulation can accommodate this behavior by sampling from the historical probability function. This is accomplished by utilizing random variables and is known as Monte Carlo sampling. Student attrition is also a stochastic process and can be effectively represented as a Markov process (Koenig).

Computer simulation is currently the only viable methodology for utilizing global models of the institution, and the state-of-the-art developments in this area (Judy; Koenig) seemingly yield more benefits in understanding and communication than in explicit problem-solving capabilities. The CAMPUS model, which

is probably the most comprehensive and successful global simulation study to date, has gained acceptance in a problem-solving
mode (Levine). At the risk of being negative about these developments, which are no doubt in a gestation period with a very
bright prognosis, it is conjectured that modeling on a smaller
scale is more judicious, yielding better payoffs and more
successes; and further, the science (or art) of institutional
modeling will evolve more rationally as a result.

Micro modeling minimizes the probability of "teetering on
the brink of witchcraft" and, indeed, often allows one to solve
the model, in the sense of selecting the best alternative
directly. The procedure is to mathematically express some
measure of subsystem performance P in terms of a manageable
set of controls C_i and uncontrolled U_j variables:

$$P = f(C_i, U_j)$$

For example, institutions generally have control over the
number of admissions C_i, but cannot control to as great an
extent the number of applications U_j. Perhaps it will also
be necessary to mathematically express some constraints on
C_i and U_j. The objective is to optimize performance (minimize
cost, maximize utilization of space, etc.) subject to the constraints. It is simply too ambitious a task at present to
attempt constructing such a model for the institution as a
whole; rather, some subsystem — physical plant, labor, store-
room inventories, classroom space, or the like — should be the
object of such a model.

Techniques are available for attacking such problems and
have been applied to analogous situations in industry, the
military, and governmental agencies. Specifically, mathematical programing, differential calculus, and the various algo-
rithms of queuing, sequencing, routing, and replacement theories
of operations research are often applicable.

The subsystem to be modeled must be manageable in the sense
that performance can be explicitly identified and the relationship between the subsystem variables can be mathematically expressed. The utility of modeling on a smaller scale rests upon
being able to overcome mathematical complexities while at the
same time not detracting to a large degree from the potential

payoff by confining attention to an insignificant problem or
by incurring subsystem suboptimization.

Recommendations for modeling

The question of what to model evokes some wide differences
of opinion, but it is possible to present the key considerations:

     1. What is value of success?

     2. What is the probability of success?

     3. How much does success cost?

The answer to the question of what to model is theoretically
simple: "Model in the area that yields the highest *expected*
value of success." The difficulty arises, of course, from
measuring value, probability, and cost of success. Rather
than offer an opinion of where the most benefits may accrue,
some recommendations are presented instead.

     1. Cast a look at the capital and operating budgets of the
institution to see where the money goes. Considering a global
budget breakdown, it looks as if instruction or research would
yield the highest potential payoff.

     2. Perform a comprehensive survey of the literature to see
what has been done and what can be used more or less directly
— and do not confine the survey to applications in education.
Physical plant operations are similar in many respects to
industrial job shops, and a high probability of success could
be expected from modeling in this area.

     3. Evaluate your institution — in terms of model building
capability, acceptance and use of the model results, data
available to define the system elements and relationships, and
commitment to the task (usually measured in terms of funds
allocated for this purpose). In order to achieve success it
is necessary to institute change and overcome the costs of
complexity. Modeling directed toward the academic staff resource scores low in this regard.

     4. Avoid building models which have to search for problems
to solve.

     5. Modeling efforts should be directed toward an analysis
of "discretionary resources." One of the initial steps should

be to identify resources which the institution can control,
since it is useless to determine "optimal levels" and then not
be able to implement or influence the associated resource
allocations.

Modeling can be an important and effective aid in higher
education administration and management if the institution can
muster faith and long-term commitment to the task and yet maintain a judicious stability (as expressed by Boguslaw, so as not
to be "wagged increasingly by its technological tail").
There is a wide gap between the state of the art of model
building in major universities and that in large corporations,
and well-managed institutions must reconcile this discrepancy
— either by identifying the underlying reasons for it by ini-
tiating efforts to eliminate it.

[Comment by the editors. *This chapter presents an excellent
overview of the basic principles of modeling and the application of the modeling approach to higher education administration and management.*

*If models are constructed which can accurately predict the
effect of alternative policies, some interesting questions will
be raised concerning the use of such models. Will this resource
be available only to the administration and perhaps the governing board? Faculty, students, and alumni have a vital stake in
the outcomes of alternate policy decisions. Can they be expected to subscribe to policies adopted as the result of using
such models, without knowledge of the predicted outcomes of the
policies adopted or of the predicted outcomes of the policies
not adopted by the controlling board or the administration?
Will concern over the answers to these questions create a
reluctance on the part of university administrators to experiment with computer models?*

*A wide gap exists between higher education and the larger
corporations in the state of the art of model building. Does
the concern with external integration, a concern so much greater
in education institutions than in industrial corporations, generate anxieties which explain the existence of this gap? One
characteristic of an effective model is that it makes decision*

criteria readily apparent. Because the university serves a
variety of publics — students, faculty, alumni, foundations,
federal agencies — with widely varying success criteria, this
characteristic may be seen as detrimental to achieving the
administrative goal of satisfying the various publics of the
university.

Although this paper is quite comprehensive, the reader interested in the use of modeling for higher education administration and management may wish to have additional information
concerning such items as the specification of discretionary
policy variables, output variables relevant to decision making,
and the functional relationships between policy variables and
output variables. For such readers a brief bibliography
follows.]

Selected bibliography for chapter 7

Ackoff, Russell L. "Management Misinformation," *Management
     Science*, vol. 14, no. 4 (Dec. 1967).
Amundsen, Richard P. "Regression Study for University Office
     of Space Programming." UADP Internal Report.
Beshers, James M. *Substantive Issues in Models of Large Scale
     Social Systems*. Cambridge, Mass., no date.
Boguslaw, Robert. *The New Utopians*. Englewood Cliffs, N.J.,
     Prentice-Hall, 1965.
Chaney, John F. "Acquisition and Management of Data for Higher
     Education Management Information Systems." Paper presented
     to the Conference on Management Information Systems: Their
     Development and Application to the Administration of Higher
     Education, sponsored by WICHE and the American Council on
     Higher Education in Washington, D.C., April 24-26, 1969.
     Proceedings to be published.
Crecine, John P. "A Computer Simulation Model of Municipal
     Budgeting," *Management Science*, vol. 13, no. 11 (July 1967).
Demski, Joel S. "Some Considerations in Sensitizing an Opti-
     mization Model," *Journal of Industrial Engineering*, vol. 19,
     no. 9 (Sept. 1968).
Elmaghraby, Salah E. "The Role of Modeling in IE Design,"
     Journal of Industrial Engineering, vol. 19, no. 6 (June
     1968).
Fain, W. W., Janice B. Fain, and H. W. Karr. "A Tactical War-
     fare Simulation Program," *Naval Research Logistics Quarterly*,
     vol. 13, no. 4 (Dec. 1966).
Fetter, R. B., and J. D. Thompson. "The Simulation of Hospital
     Systems," *Operations Research*, vol. 13, no. 5 (Sept.-Oct.
     1965).
Flores, Dagoberto. "Some Questions on Higher Education Plan-
     ning." UADP Internal Report.

Judy, Richard W. "Systems Analysis for Efficient Resource Allocation in Higher Education." Paper presented to the Conference on Management Information Systems: Their Development and Application to the Administration of Higher Education, sponsored by WICHE and the American Council on Higher Education in Washington, D.C., April 24-26, 1969. Proceedings to be published.

Judy, Richard W., and Jack B. Levine. "The Integration of Simulation Models and Program Budgeting in University Planning and Administration." Paper presented at the Joint ORSA/TIMS Meeting, San Francisco, May 1968.

Keller, John. "Higher Education Objectives: Measures of Performance and Effectiveness." Paper presented to the Conference on Management Information Systems: Their Development and Application to the Administration of Higher Education, sponsored by WICHE and the American Council on Higher Education in Washington, D.C., April 24-26, 1969. Proceedings to be published.

Kilbridge, Maurice, Robert P. O'Block, and Paul V. Teplitz. "A Conceptual Framework for Urban Planning Models," *Management Science*, vol. 15, no. 6 (Feb. 1969).

Koenig, Herman E. "A Systems Model for Management Planning and Resource Allocation in Institutions of Higher Education." Paper presented to the Conference on Management Information Systems: Their Development and Application to the Administration of Higher Education, sponsored by WICHE and the American Council on Higher Education in Washington, D.C., April 24-26, 1969. Proceedings to be published.

Levine, Jack B. "The Implementation of CAMPUS Simulation Models for University Planning." Paper presented to the Conference on Management Information Systems: Their Development and Application to the Administration of Higher Education, sponsored by WICHE and the American Council on Higher Education in Washington, D.C., April 24-26, 1969. Proceedings to be published.

Levine, Jack B. "Application of the CAMPUS Simulation Models to the Major Planning Decisions of a Large University." Paper presented at the ACM Conference, New York, 1969.

McKenney, James L. "Critique of 'Verification of Computer Simulation Models'", *Management Science*, vol. 14, no. 2 (Oct. 1967).

McMillan, Claude, and R. F. Gonzales. *Systems Analysis*, rev. ed., Homewood, Ill., Irwin, 1968.

Mize, Joe H., and J. Grady Cox. "Essentials of Simulation Models for University Planning."

Naylor, Thomas H., and J. M. Finger. "Verification of Computer Simulation Models," *Management Science*, vol. 14, no. 2 (Oct. 1967).

Naylor, Thomas H., Joseph L. Balintfy, Donald F. Burdick, and Kong Chu. *Computer Simulation Techniques*, New York, Wiley, 1966.

Editors' bibliography

Cohen, Kalman J., and others. *Carnegie Tech Management Game*, Homewood, Ill., Irwin, 1964.

EDUCOM, Bulletin of the Interuniversity Communications Council, Jan. 1968.

Evans, G., and others. *Simulation Using Digital Computers*,
    Englewood Cliffs, N.J., Prentice-Hall, 1967.
Greenlawn, Paul S., and others. *Business Simulation in Indust-
    rial and University Education*, Englewood Cliffs, N.J.,
    Prentice-Hall, 1962.
Henshaw, Richard C., and J. R. Jackson. *Executive Game*, Home-
    wood, Ill., Irwin, 1966.
Herron, Lowell W. *Executive Action Simulation*, Englewood Cliffs,
    N.J., Prentice-Hall.
Judy, Richard W., and Jack B. Levine. *A New Tool for Educational
    Administrators: A Report to the Commission on the Financing
    of Higher Education*, Toronto, University of Toronto Press,
    1965.
Judy, R. W., B. L. Hansen, W. G. Wolfson, and S. I. Centner.
    *Analysis of the Effects of Formula Financing on Ontario
    Universities*, Office of Institutional Research, AIR-4,
    University of Toronto, 1966.
Judy, R. W. *Data Requirements of the CAMPUS Model*, Office of
    Institutional Research, OIR-1, University of Toronto, 1966.
Judy, R. W. *Source of Numeric Parameter Values for CAMPUS*,
    Office of Institutional Research, OIR-3, University of
    Toronto, 1966.
Judy, R. W. *Simulation and Rational Resource Allocation in
    Universities*. Paper given at the meeting of Ad Hoc Group
    on Efficiency in Resource Utilization in Education, O.E.C.D.,
    Paris, France, Jan. 1967.
Judy, R. W. *Systems Analysis and University Planning*. Paper
    presented at the Symposium on Operations Analysis of Educa-
    tion, Washington, D.C., Nov. 1967.
Judy, R. W. *Economic Analysis in University Planning*. Paper
    presented at the Annual Meeting of the Canadian Economics
    Association, Calgary, Alta., June 1968.
Judy, R. W. *Educational Planning with Simulation Analysis*.
    Paper presented at the Colleges of Applied Arts and Techno-
    logy Design Workshop, University of Waterloo, Waterloo,
    Ontario, 1968.
Judy, R. W. "Simulation Aids College Plan," *Canadian University*,
    Nov. 1968.
Levine, Jack B., and Richard W. Judy. "Techniques of Systems
    Analysis for University Planning and Administration,"
    chapters in *Handbook of College and University Administra-
    tors*, ed. A. S. Knowles, New York, McGraw Hill, 1969.
Levine, Jack B., Richard W. Judy, John R. Walter, and Richard
    Wilson, M.D. *Systems Analysis of Alternative Designs of a
    Faculty*. Paper given at the meeting of Budgeting, Program
    Analysis and Cost Effectiveness in Educational Planning,
    O.E.C.D., Paris, France, April 1968.
Levine, J. B., and R. W. Judy. Chapters describing case-study
    applications of CAMPUS in *Practical Uses of Cost Analysis
    to Improve Educational Planning*, to be published in 1969 by
    International Institute for Educational Planning, Paris,
    France.
McKenney, J. L. *Simulation Gaming for Management Development*.
    Cambridge, Mass., Harvard Business School, 1967.
Martin, E. Wain, Jr. *Management Decision Simulation*, Homewood,
    Ill., Irwin, 1961.
Pfeiffer, John. *New Look at Education: Systems Analysis in Our
    Schools and Colleges*, New York, Odyssey, 1968.

Rath, Gustave J. "Management Science" in *University Operation* 14, no. 6 (Feb. 1968).
Vance, Stanley. *Management Decision Simulation*, New York, McGraw-Hill, 1960.

Chapter eight. The impact of academic program structure on the utilization of space and time resources of colleges and universities: a research model. *F. William Arcuri, Thomas R. Mason, and Mark Meredith*

Purpose of the study

The purpose of this study was to model mathematically the impact of academic program structure upon the utilization of resources of instructional time and space.

Essentially, the study provides evidence of the extent to which differences in the composition and structure of academic programs among institutions of different types affect scheduling capability and therefore the degree to which their instructional facilities may be scheduled at a high level of utilization.

The purpose of the model is to permit the measurement of certain characteristics of academic programs — rates of student course enrollments, class size distribution, curriculum structure — in relation to the utilization of space and time resources. The study is highly theoretical and mathematically abstracted from a complex reality, and it does not undertake to solve the problem of academic program scheduling. Without this degree of abstraction, the measurement of these relationships would have been swamped by the multitude of subtle and idiosyncratic factors involved in the real world of academic program scheduling.

Although a broader purpose of the study was to attempt to find ways of measuring the differential instructional space utilization capabilities of colleges and universities of different types and sizes, the limited scope of this study did not permit any exact determination of how such a method might be achieved. The study showed great promise, however, for ultimately discovering means of assessing variable space-utilization capacities as a function of program structure.

The study provides additional evidence that statewide or systemwide norms of space utilization, applicable to institutions of all types without regard to differences in academic program, are seriously in error. The importance of this knowledge is emphasized by the fact that in many states simple measures of classroom utilization carry much weight in establishing priorities for capital-fund allocations to college and university building projects. Many of the norms or standards applied by state agencies to capital projects for higher education have been pirated from other states which originally picked them out of the air, selected them from incomplete compilations of "normative" data, or invented them by seat-of-the-pants guesswork. None of these "standards" is based on a thorough study of the nature of the factors — and they are extremely complex — which determine a valid level of utilization capability

This study (1) makes a beginning toward a more rational means of determining criteria of space utilization for a given institution, based on the unique characteristics of its academic program, and (2) demonstrates the power of mathematical modeling as an aid to improving scheduling systems and thus improving the effectiveness of instruction.

Study approach and premises

This study grew out of the experience of one of the authors, Arcuri, with the application of a graph-theory model to the computer scheduling of examinations. Arcuri had developed a successful program for scheduling final examinations to minimize student exam conflicts, minimize sequential exams, and minimize the number of exam periods required. He had applied this model to a number of institutions in the Rochester area. Significant differences among institutions were observed in the number of examination periods required to achieve a zero-conflict schedule. It appeared that these differences were a function of differences in the patterns of student course enrollments and program structures.

Arcuri called these phenomena to the attention of Mason and Meredith, whose work in facilities planning had brought them up against the problem of utilization criteria as a factor in

predicting classroom and teaching laboratory requirements for
colleges and universities.

Further investigation indicated that three factors were of
importance in affecting differences in scheduling capability:
(1) the number of courses in which each student was enrolled,
(2) the size of the course or course section, and (3) the degree
of prescribed or lock-step curriculum in the institution's program.

Assisted by a grant from the Esso Education Foundation and
with further assistance from the University of Rochester, a
computer program was developed to apply the graph model (described below) to the general problem of student-course scheduling in search of measures of scheduling capability (degrees
of scheduling difficulty and degrees of scheduling flexibility)
as a function of academic program structure.

Three hypotheses can be deduced from the graph model:

1. Scheduling flexibility varies inversely with the average
   course enrollments per student.
2. Scheduling flexibility varies inversely with the average
   number of students in each course or section.
3. Scheduling flexibility varies directly with the degree
   of prescribed or lock-step curriculum.

Scheduling flexibility is viewed as instrumental to a higher
level of utilization of instructional space and time.

The general approach of the study was as follows. The input
to the graph model is the institution's file of student requests
for courses. Only an identifying number for each student and
for each course or course section is required as data input to
the generalized model. The model measures the interconnections
among students and courses, among courses through each student
enrolling in them, and among students through the courses in
which they enroll. The degrees of interconnection produce the
measures of structure (rates of course enrollments, average
class sizes, and degree of prescribed curriculum) and the
measures of scheduling capability. The model and the nature of
these measures are explained more fully below.

This is a highly idealized model of the scheduling process.
Even though the data are from real files of student requests
for courses in real institutions, the model ignores many of

the real-world constraints that face the registrar or scheduling officer. There was no attempt, within the limited scope
of this study, to account for the actual existing room inventory
by type and size or the real weekly time-period inventory of
the institutions studied. Nor was there an attempt to account
for those very crucial real-world constraints — the time preferences of faculty and students.

The model is capable of being encumbered with such constraints
as room type and size, Professor Buzzfuzz's insistence on teaching only at 10 a.m. MWF, and the weekly timetable structure of
the institution. However, the objective was not to build an
operating scheduling system. It was to use the theoretical
model of scheduling as a tool of analysis to understand the
interaction of students and courses in varying academic programs
and to show how these variations are likely to affect scheduled
utilization of instructional facilities. Applied to a real
room-and-time inventory, the model could provide a powerful
tool in improving the scheduling. However, the addition of a
multitude of real-world constraints so greatly increases the
complexity of the model that a great deal of effort would have
to be expended to bring it to a point where it could supply an
operational system of schedule building or schedule planning in
a college or university.

The data sources were files of student requests for courses
for one term from ten educational units in the Rochester area.
The ten institutional programs were selected on the basis of
availability of data, rather than any structured sample of
institutional types. However, the cases do represent a highly
diversified group of academic program activities, with a wide
range of variance in the measures of program structure. The
course request files used were (1) the 3,500-student undergraduate program of the University of Rochester; (2) the East-
man School of Music, an autonomous program of conservatory type;
(3) the day program of Rochester Institute of Technology, a
3,200-student program with a highly prescribed curriculum of
applied arts and technology; (4) the evening program of Rochester
Institute of Technology, mainly for part-time students; (5) a
1,000-student four-year liberal arts college for men; (6) a
1,200-student liberal arts college for women; (7) a large, urban

junior college; (8) a small liberal arts college for men; and
(9 and 10) two regional, semirural high schools.

In some cases, the course-request files involved registration
for course sections and in other cases for entire courses. This
introduced a wide range in class size, depending on whether the
size was that of a section in a multisection course, or was that
of the total enrollment. For evaluating the numerical properties
in the model, this difference does not matter. The files in
which the requests are for courses, rather than sections, are
merely viewed as programs with very large class sizes.

In addition to applying the data from the ten programs to the
model, an in-depth study was done of the University of Rochester
River Campus instructional program (both undergraduate and graduate), to assess the effects on the scheduling measures of the
different levels of instruction.

The graph model

For purposes of explanation, the graph model is divided into
two parts: the enrollments graph and the associations graph.

The enrollments graph describes the relationship of students
to sections for a given institution or educational unit. Each
student or section is represented by a small circle (a node or
vertex). Each association between a student and a section is
shown by a connecting line (branch or edge), the interconnections
occurring at the nodes. The nodes of this graph are of two
classes: one class corresponds to the students of the modeled
institution; the other class corresponds to its sections. The
branches of this graph connecting student nodes to section nodes
correspond to the institution's section enrollments.

To illustrate the enrollments graph, consider a hypothetical
institution whose academic program involves 4 students enrolling
in 4 sections in the manner shown in Table 3.

Two fundamental numeric properties of graphs are order and
degree. The order of a graph is the number of nodes in the
graph, and the degree of a node is the number of branches inci-
dent to that node.

Table 3. *Student programs*

Student 1	Student 2	Student 3	Student 4
Section A	Section A	Section B	Section B
Section B	Section B	Section C	Section C
	Section C	Section D	Section D
	Section D		

The enrollments graph for this example is illustrated in Figure 3.

The values and interpretations of these fundamental measures applied to the enrollments graph (Figure 3 are tabulated in Table 4.

Table 4. *Enrollments graph*

Node	Degree	Interpretation	Node	Degree	Interpretation
1	2	Student 1 section load is 2	A	2	Section size of A is 2
2	4	Student 2 section load is 4	B	4	Section size of B is 4
3	3	Student 3 section load is 3	C	3	Section size of C is 3
4	3	Student 4 section load is 3	D	3	Section size of D is 3

Order	Interpretation	Order	Interpretation
4	No. of students is 4	4	No. of sections is 4

The associations graph, like the enrollments graph, consists of nodes of the two classes — students and sections — and describes the degree of association between pairs of students and pairs of sections for a given institution. Unlike the enrollments graph, however, the branches of this graph connect only nodes of the same class. Two nodes connected in this manner are said to be "associated" and any branches which connect them are called "associations."

The number of associations for any pair of student nodes is the number of section enrollments that the two students have in common; the number of associations for any pair of section nodes is the number of students that the two sections have in common. (Note that any pair of associated sections generated by a student enrolling in both sections is considered to be in potential conflict and that those two sections must be scheduled at different times.)

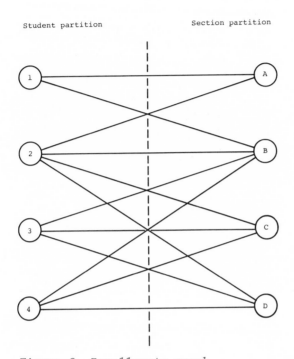

Figure 3. *Enrollments graph*

The values and intepretations of the fundamental measure of degree as applied to the associations graph are tabulated in Table 5.

Table 5. *Associations graph*

Node	Degree	Interpretation	Node	Degree	Interpretation
1	4	Student 1 has 4 associations	A	4	Section A has 4 associations
2	8	Student 2 has 8 associations	B	8	Section B has 8 associations
3	7	Student 3 has 7 associations	C	7	Section C has 7 associations
4	7	Student 4 has 7 associations	D	7	Section D has 7 associations

Student partition   Section partition

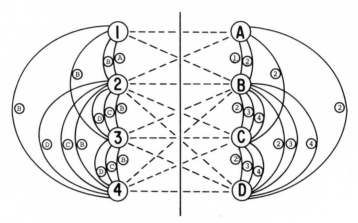

Figure 4. *Associations graph*

The relationships of both the enrollments graph and the associations graph are established in the computer storage in the form of an incidence matrix of students to sections, a binary measure identifying whether each particular student or section is associated or not. A simple illustration of this matrix, from which are derived the associations of students and sections in the hypothetical example, is given in Figure 5. The same matrix is shown twice: first, to indicate the student course loads and section sizes of the enrollments graph and, secondly to identify student and section associations in the associations graph.

The final component related to the graph model is the room-time logical inventory. This inventory consists of a graphic portrayal of the rooms available for scheduling course sections at a given institution times the number of weekly hours that are allocated for scheduled instruction. An illustrative room-time inventory is shown in Figure 6.

In summary, these are the components used to model the enrollment process and, aided by computer programs, to then identify and measure (a) certain dimensions of the academic program structure, (b) the impact of such structure upon scheduling capability and hence the utilization of resources of

instructional time and space, and (c) variations in these
dimensions of program structure between institutions.

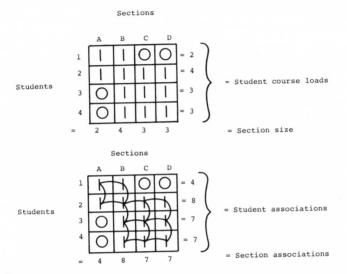

Figure 5. *An incidence matrix: above, showing
the order of the enrollments graph; below,
showing the degree of the associations graph*

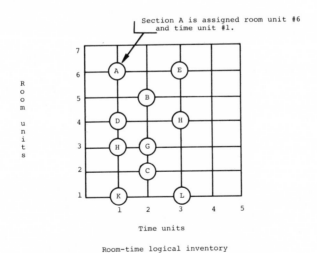

Figure 6. *Room-time logical inventory*

The measures created in the study are called affinity, density, and mobility. Other measures used are student course-section load and section size.

Affinity is a measure of the degree of association between any pair of students or pair of sections. It is a measure taken from the associations graph and is defined for any pair of nodes, say A and B, as the number of branches between A and divided by the degree of A or the degree of B, whichever is smaller. (For percentage affinity this quantity is multiplied by 100.) We call this measure "student affinity" if it is determined for a pair of student nodes and "section affinity" if it is determined for a pair of section nodes.

As an example, suppose that section X has 20 enrollments, section Y has 50 enrollments, and sections X and Y have 5 students in common. Affinity would be measured as follows:

Section X	20
Section Y	50
Students in both	5
Affinity	5/20 = 0.25

This measure reflects in part the degree of prescription in the curriculum of the institution to which it is applied; that is, as the degree of curriculum prescription is increased, the average degree of association (affinity) is increased. For computational considerations mainly, section affinity was chosen to reflect the degree of prescription in the curriculum of the institutions used in this comparison, i.e., the degree to which groups of students are taking the same courses in common patterns.

Density is a measure of the frequency of incidence of association (i.e., potential conflict) of a given section with all other sections to be scheduled. It is a measure derived from a section-to-section incidence matrix and is defined as the sum of the incidences of association for any section divided by the total number of sections.

A section association density of 100 percent would indicate that a particular section is associated with every other section. A 50 percent density would indicate association with half of the other sections. This measure is a good indicator of scheduling

difficulty; that is, as the density increases the scheduling
difficulty usually increases. This measure, however, is very
sensitive to institution size and can be misleading when comparing institutions which vary widely in this regard.

Mobility is a measure of the interaction of section activities in time and indicates the relative degree of flexibility
available to an institution for scheduling its instructional
program. This is, perhaps, the most important of the measures
derived from the graphs. It is determined by identifying the
number of room-times needed to schedule courses free of student-
course conflict and subtracting this number from the total room-
time inventory that the institution has, leaving a balance in
which to schedule courses with the least or no student-course
conflict.

The relationship of this interaction to facilities utilization can be viewed as follows. Consider that a general-purpose
inventory of room and time unit resources is available for scheduling; that is, any room-and-time-unit pair (see Figure 5) can
be assigned to any arbitrary section activity. Next, a set of
section activities is defined as "completely associated" if every
pair of sections in that set is associated. The order of such a
set is the number of sections in that set. Finally, the "maximum
completely associated set" of section activities for a particular
section is defined as the completely associated set with maximum
order which contains that section.

When scheduling a particular section activity into a room-
and-time-unit pair, the freedom of scheduling is related to how
that section interacts in time with the other sections which
have to be scheduled. Suppose, for example, that section A is
not associated with any other section to be scheduled. In such
a case, the choice of a time unit for section A is unrestricted.
Alternatively, suppose that section A is associated with two
other associated sections B and C. Since sections B and C are
associated they must be scheduled in separate time units, and
since section A is associated with both, one can consider that
at least two time units are unavailable for scheduling section
A. By definition, sections A, B, and C form a completely
associated set of order 3. Consider further that section A is
also a member of a completely associated set of order greater

than 3. Suppose the order of the maximum completely associated
set containing section A is 10. Then, in the same sense as
before, 9 time unit blocks will be unavailable for scheduling
section A. If the total number of general purpose time unit
blocks available for scheduling all sections is 15 (e.g., 15
time blocks of 3 periods each in a 45-hour week) then 15 minus
9, or 6 time unit blocks would be available for scheduling
section A. Another way of viewing this is to say that 6/15 or
40 percent of the logical inventory is available for scheduling
section A. We refer to this quantity as "section mobility."

Section mobility may be viewed as a measure of scheduling
flexibility. An institution with high section mobility should
be able to adapt with ease its real schedule of courses to
realistic operating constraints — time preferences of student
and faculty, room sizes, and room characteristics. An institution with low section mobility will have more difficulty adapt-
ing its schedule to such constraints.

These key measures as averages are recapitulated in Table 6.

Table 6.

Average section load	The average number of course-section enrollments per student.
Average section size	The average number of students enrolled per section.
Average affinity	The average degree of association between sections.
Average density	The average incidence of associa-tion between sections.
Average mobility	The average degree of scheduling flexibility available to an in-structional program.

Test results

The measures from test runs of the ten institutional files
of student course requests against the graph model are summar-
ized in Table 7, arranged in ascending order of average section
density.

The three structure measures — course load, section size,
and affinity — are not independent of one another. They interact to affect the degree of difficulty (density) and flexibility

(mobility) of the theoretical scheduling capability. The compounding of high course loads, high class sizes, and low section affinity to affect scheduling capability is such that a much larger number of cases would be required to apply formal multivariate analysis in a meaningful way. Hence, the evaluation of the factors affecting scheduling capability, at this stage, is limited to observational assessment.

Table 7. *Rochester graph model measures of ten institutional instructional programs (in order of average section density)*

		Structure measures			Scheduling measures	
Institution	No. of course sections	Average section load	Average section size	Average affinity	Average section density	Average section mobility
A	298	4.5	49.0	23.7	5.3	60.5
*B	205	7.9	24.1	57.5	9.5	31.8
C	129	2.2	27.0	8.7	12.5	67.5
D	359	3.8	38.1	9.2	12.5	51.6
E	277	4.8	15.5	16.7	13.1	41.3
F	253	5.3	26.9	13.0	15.9	25.2
G	123	4.1	46.7	18.3	19.9	45.0
H	109	4.1	113.7**	18.3	27.2	27.5
I	118	5.1	43.8	14.6	32.8	19.8
*J	133	8.7	60.3**	26.1	38.8	6.0

*Institutions B and J are high schools.
**The request files for H and J are for courses rather than class sections. This explains the high values for average section size.

In any case, the interaction of the variables in the model is to a large extent logically determinable. The more courses a student enrolls in, the more other courses he will bring into association (or conflict) with each other. The more students enrolled in a single course, the more other courses are brought into association (or conflict) with that course. The more extensive the degree to which students enroll in common course patterns (e.g., as a result of a highly prescribed curriculum), the less difficult it will be for these courses to be ordered into a time frame (once one student has brought two courses into conflict, additional students enrolling in the same pair of courses make no difference in the density of the sections association matrix, and the degree of potential association or conflict is relatively decreased by the increase in common course-enrollment patterns of larger numbers of students).

These deductions could be empirically confirmed with a larger number of test cases than were applied in this study.

A visual representation of the test cases is offered in the bar charts of Figures 7 and 8; the originals for these were computer-produced. Figure 7 shows the structure measures against average section density. Figure 8 graphs the same structure measures in relation to average section mobility. Note that bars B and J represent high schools, which tend to have deviant patterns compared with the college programs tested.

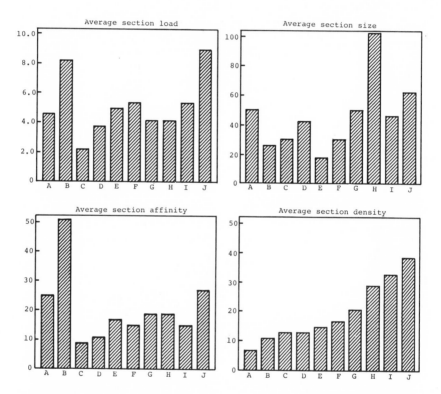

Figure 7. *APSA comparative summary B and J represent high schools*

Among the observable characteristics of the test data, the following are noteworthy.

As an example of prescribed curriculum, the Rochester Institute of Technology day program (institution A) showed a measure of extraordinarily high affinity. It has by far the lowest density of course conflicts and a very high mobility; therefore, it should have a more flexible scheduling problem. The high affinity of its prescribed program substantially offsets the fact that RIT has relatively high student course loads and relatively high class sizes.

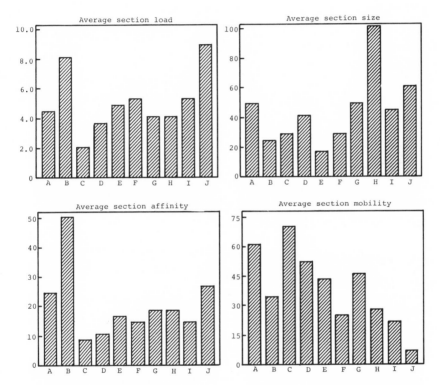

Figure 8. *APSA comparative summary B and J represent high schools*

As an illustration of the effect of average course load on density and mobility, the University of Rochester's under-graduate program (institution D) is a four-course program com-pared with the typical five or six courses per full-time student in most of the other programs. This lower average course load significantly offsets the fact that the University of Rochester has a highly unprescribed and open curriculum that results in low affinity.

Although the observable tendencies of the test cases generally confirm the hypotheses, a considerably larger sample of institutional cases will be required before the relative weight of the structural measures can be analyzed and possibly used as a predictive aid in scheduling or in the weighting of utilization criteria.

To gain another perspective on the problem, the graph model was applied to the University of Rochester River Campus program divided by level of instruction. The measures of average class size and average section affinity could be juxtaposed against average section density. Table 8 shows the outcomes for the College of Arts and Science.

Table 8. *University of Rochester College of Arts and Science: APSA test case — instructional load*

Course level*	Type	Enrollment	Number of sections	Average section size	Average section affinity	Average section density
100's	CLR	6725	151	44.5	11.4	10.5
200's	CLR	4231	140	30.2	15.8	6.8
300's	CLR	89	14	6.3	25.9	1.6
400's	CLR	437	44	9.9	38.2	1.4
500's	CLR	614	87	7.0	44.6	0.7
All	CLR	12096	436	27.7	22.6	6.2

*Course levels: Courses numbered in the 100's are taken by freshmen and sophomores, courses in the 200's by juniors and seniors, courses in the 300's by honors students and courses in the 400's and 500's by graduate students.

As the level of course rises from freshman-sophomore (100's) through advanced graduate (500's), the section sizes decline sharply, as would be expected. At the same time section affinity rises rapidly as level increases. The compounding of the two brings a radical drop in the average section density, the density of potential student-course conflicts.

Affinity rises because (1) as the level of course increases, section size generally decreases, and (2) students enrolled in lower-division undergraduate programs have much more diversified programs, but as the level of the course advances, the upper division and graduate concentration creates a higher degree of common course patterns among advanced students. This would imply that institutions with a greater proportion of advanced undergraduate and graduate programs (programs with high operating costs) are easier to accommodate in a scheduling situation and would contribute to the higher rates of utilization observed in larger universities compared with smaller, liberal arts programs.

The relationship of class size to scheduling density is further illustrated in Table 9. Here, the University of Rochester data are arranged by class size intervals, and the average density rises acutely.

Table 9. *University of Rochester College of Arts and Science: APSA test case — instructional space; type CLR*

Size	Density	Room hours	Size	Density	Room hours
1-10	1.2	513.0	61- 80	16.6	45.0
11-20	4.0	208.0	81-100	19.5	6.0
21-30	7.5	231.0	101-150	24.2	18.0
31-40	9.3	90.0	151-250	29.0	30.0
41-60	11.8	97.0	Over 250	37.1	15.0

Conclusions

It is evident that the factors influencing an institution's scheduling capability, and hence the levels at which it may utilize its instructional facilities, are complexly interrelated. These relationships have yet to be untangled, but they point to the possibilities of finding ways of predicting the effective levels of space utilization for individual institutions or, at least, providing weighting factors for utilization norms or standards that account for differences among institutions.

As for policy implications, this study confirms what many institutional administrators and specialists in space planning and scheduling have been saying for a long time; that is, the allocation of capital resources should not depend on the homogeneous ranking of different institutions and their projects according to simple, uniform measures of instructional space utilization.

Note

This chapter is a report on research sponsored by the Esso Education Foundation and the University of Rochester, prepared for the Esso Education Foundation Seminar on Management Information Systems in Higher Education, Duke University, June 24-27, 1969.

Three papers given before the 55th Annual Meeting of the American Association of Collegiate Registrars and Admissions Officers, Dallas, April 1969, focus on the policy issues of space utilization. They are Thomas R. Mason's, "The Impact of Academic Program Structure on Instructional Space Utilization," a companion to this chapter that focuses on the historical and policy issues of instructional space utilization; Donovan Smith's, "Optimal Class Scheduling," which argues that excessively high utilization is uneconomic when instructional and other costs are accounted for; and H. D. Bareither's, "Theoretical Maximum Scheduling and Utilization of Classrooms." These are to be published in the *Proceedings* of the AACRAO meeting in *College and University*.

Chapter nine. A simulation modeling approach to a scheduling problem. *Clark R. Cahow, Joe McDonald, and Roger Wilkins*

The scheduling problem at Duke University

For the past two years Duke University has been working toward the development of techniques to improve the utilization of its resources. The area of activity which has received the greatest concentration of effort has been the scheduling system. In the face of pressures arising from expanding enrollments as well as increased and enriched course offerings, more and more attention has been focused on the scheduling system which must perform the function of allocating scarce resources (classroom space and faculty time) to increasing student demand.

All of the research completed thus far has centered on the scheduling system as it currently exists at Duke, with the following general kinds of questions in mind:

1. Will the scheduling system as it now exists continue to function in a changing environment?
2. Are certain types of policy changes feasible under the current scheduling system? If so, what are the effects of such policy changes? Are the results acceptable or desirable?
3. Can the scheduling system be altered to improve the utilization of resources?

The examination of questions such as these and the research which has followed has been and will continue to be carried out in the light of the general philosophy underlying scheduling at Duke; to wit, each student warrants the opportunity to choose his courses and instructors in a way that promotes his individual concept of an optimum learning experience. At the same time, the need is recognized for providing the best possible teaching schedule for the instructor so that he can combine teaching, student contact, and research hours in an acceptable manner.

This is the point which differentiates the research efforts
at Duke from those being carried on at other institutions.
At some, the scheduling problem resolved is one in which (1)
students are allowed to select only the course; the instructor
and time sequence are assigned from a prestructured schedule
of courses, or (2) students request courses and a general schedule is structured for both students and faculty.

The problem at Duke can be viewed as the problem of trying
to maximize two separate sets of utility or preference functions
where these two functions are in conflict. At some point trade-
offs must be made between the two.

The problem created by attempting to serve the needs of both
students and faculty at Duke was not severe as long as there
were ample facilities to allow schedule adjustments at registration, when sufficient faculty and space were on hand to provide numerous small sections and a variety of meeting times for
courses; and when a comparatively simple structure of courses
was available to the student. Now, however, with expanding enrollment and the creation of more complex course structures,
the present system of ad hoc scheduling by departments tends
to force a rigid schedule that makes it more difficult to match
student demand with faculty availability. The combination of
these and other factors causes an overload on facilities, an
imbalance between populated and underpopulated classes, and too
many multisectioned courses if an attempt is made to provide
students with a wide variety of choices for both time and instructors. The problem has become even more critical at Duke
due to proposed changes in curriculum and other factors which
directly affect the role of scheduling in the university.

There are basically two classes of policy change which will
affect the scheduling system: (1) *Curriculum* and curriculum-
related changes, e.g., changing the student's course load requirement or expansion of tutorial and independent study programs; and (2) *schedule* changes, e.g., changing the time
structure in which classes will meet.

In examining the effects of potential administrative policies
and decision rules, Duke has opted for a computer simulation
approach. The advantage of this approach is that, with a
simulation model, experiments can be performed which test the

effects of alternative policies and decision rules on the
behavior of the system. It is believed that this type of
experimentation will allow evaluation of new policies before
they are put into effect.

In determining the research requirements for constructing
a simulated environment which will allow experimentation with
the two general classes of policy change (i.e., curriculum and
schedule) the need was seen for two types of simulation models.
The first is a general model in which departmental course
offerings are combined into a master course schedule. A student
demand for this schedule is forecast on an aggregate basis.
This model was primarily designed to test curriculum and other
general policy changes.

The second model is a micro model in the sense that student
requests and working schedules are treated on an individual
basis. This model is designed to test the effect of changes
in schedule-related policies or decision rules. The idea behind
this model is that individual student requests are given, and
working schedules are produced, under alternative scheduling
policies.

The Duke University Scheduling Test Model for Policy Simulation

DUSTMOPS (Duke University Scheduling Test Model for Policy
Simulation) is the outcome of Duke's research efforts at developing a capability for evaluating the changes in policy which
affect the scheduling system. The model is based on the following assumptions.

1. The individual departments maintain complete discretion
(within the framework of scheduling rules) in determining what
courses are to be offered, the number of sections of each course
to be offered, instructor assignments, and time assignments.

2. Students maintain their traditional right to request
course, instructor, and time preference in accordance with the
master schedule of course offerings.

3. The administration determines how the scarce resources of
time and space are allocated to the departments and how space
in course sections is allocated to student demand.

The scheduling system consists of three major centers of control (or sectors) which interact to produce a master schedule of courses and student enrollment which is, in effect, a statement of how classroom space and faculty teaching hours are allocated to student course demand.

The three major sectors of the scheduling system are well known:

1. The administrative sector is the source of scheduling policy and includes all activities performed by the scheduling committee and the registrar's office.

2. The departmental sector includes all of the activities of the individual departments in determining course offerings, instructor assignments, meeting times, and the like.

3. The student sector is viewed as one aggregate unit from which total demand for each course and section in the master schedule arises.

The general simulation model of the scheduling system consists of the simulation of these three sectors. Feedback loops between the sectors are provided logically in the model (see Figure 9).

Administrative sector.   The simulation of the administrative sector consists primarily of a logical description of the scheduling policies provided for the particular experiment being performed.   There are several bookkeeping tasks, such as balancing sections and adjusting the master schedule, which are performed by the registrar's office and are represented in this sector of the model.   Changes in policy and in scheduling procedure are reflected in this submodel by making appropriate changes in the logic of the simulated administrative sector.

Student sector.   The simulation of the student sector consists of forecasting student demand for a given simulated master course schedule.   The forecasting model is based on historical request data in accordance with certain hypotheses relative to the nature of course and section demands.

The research conducted thus far with regard to forecasting student demand has led to the following hypotheses:

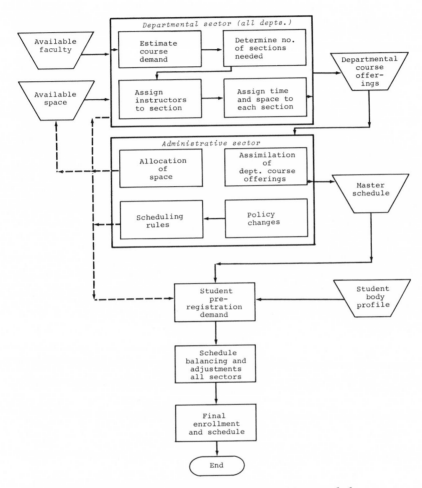

Figure 9. *Logic of the general scheduling model*

1. Course demand (defined as requests for all sections of a multi-section course) is fairly constant from year to year.

2. Course-section demand (defined as requests for a specific section of a course) will vary from year to year depending upon the instructor, meeting time, and meeting place of the section as well as the number of sections of the course offered.

Another factor which may influence course-section demand is the amount of affinity in the master course schedule. For example, if certain students normally take two single-section courses in the same semester and if these two single-section courses are scheduled in the same time period, then demand for both of these course sections will be dampened.

3. A large percentage of the enrollment in any given course is made up of a few types of students (categorized by college, major, and class).

4. Students request specific sections of a course on the basis of certain "section appeal" factors: first, "instructor appeal," and then "meeting time appeal" — the desirability of meeting time in itself and also its value in avoiding conflicts; if certain sections of a course are in conflict with other high-affinity courses, demand will gravitate towards nonconflicting sections. There is also some "meeting place appeal." This may not be a large factor, but will be influential when time and distance must be considered.

5. Students of similar academic interests and seniority (i.e., college, major, and class) will tend to request similar courses.

Our existing theory for course demand is based on the hypothesis that certain time patterns exist for course requests. After a student enters the university he chooses (at some point in time) his curriculum and major. The determination of these brings about a set of requirements (both curriculum and major) which must be satisfied prior to graduation. Moreover, the student must satisfy the overall degree requirement of some minimum number of courses (the total of the required courses and electives). There are, of course, degrees of freedom among required courses so that a quasi-continuum of the degree of choice exists between the two extremes of absolute requirements and absolute electives.

It is hypothesized that as students progress through the university from fall semester of the freshman year to spring semester of the senior year, certain patterns exist for selecting courses (both required and elective). Furthermore, it is contended that these patterns are identifiable by student type. This is not to say that all students of a given college, class, and major will request the same courses during the same semester. Rather, the assertion is that large percentages of students of certain types will tend to make similar requests. If these percentages can be identified and if they account for a major portion of the total requests made by the various student types, then a good forecast of course demand (as defined above) will be feasible.

By way of definition a "student type" is a group of students who have a common college, major, and class. Under the present method of classification the entire undergraduate student body consists of 345 distinct student types.

Findings thus far show that for any given course, the total number of requests made for that course consists largely of requests made by students from a few of these student types. Said another way, for most courses 10 to 15 student types account for 80 to 100 percent of the total requests made for a given course. The students of the different student types in the top ten for a given course represent certain percentages of the total number of students of their respective student types enrolled in the university during any given semester. The percentage of the total number of students of the student types in the top ten types who request a given course will be important for forecasting demand for that course.

Since each course has a different top ten and each section of the course has a different instructor, time, and meeting place, it will be necessary to find a different "estimating equation" for every course section in the master schedule.

With an adequate data base and without changes in the course-requirement structure it would be possible to attack the forecasting problem with a multivariate regression analysis approach. However, data are available for only four years. If regression analysis is used, the parameters of the regression equation will be found for each course, using the following explanatory variables.

1. The number of students of each student type enrolled in the university for each time period. Only the student types in the top ten would be included as variables in the estimating equation.

2. The appeal indices for time, meeting place, and instructor. These indices can be calculated from historical data. The dependent variable will be course-section demand.

Since the data base consists of data for only four years, a more heuristic procedure has been adopted. It consists of the following steps:

1. Identify the top ten for each course.
2. For each student type in the top ten calculate the historical percentage of total course requests which is represented by requests from that student type.
3. For each student type in the top ten calculate the historical percentage of all students of that student type who request the course.
4. Calculate the residual (or "other") request percentage not explained by requests from the top ten.

The demand forecast for a given course will proceed as follows.

1. Estimate the total number of students enrolled in the university for each student type in the top ten.
2. Apply the historical percentages of all students of each of the student types to arrive at the estimate of the number of requests arising from each of the top ten types.
3. Sum the estimated requests from each of the student types in the top ten.
4. Estimate the number of requests arising from the other (non-top-ten) category, using the historical other percentage for that course.
5. Total request estimates from all categories.

The forecasting procedure given above yields an estimate of total course demand. The way in which this demand is distributed among the sections of a given course depends upon the relative attractiveness of the instructors, times, and meeting places of the individual sections. These measures of attractiveness are historical indices calculated on a cross-sectional

basis. They are indices of requests made for time periods,
instructors, and meeting places as percentages of total requests.

It is true that the heuristic approach chosen is based on
the same data base as regression analysis would be, but it
allows for several possibilities:

1. Examination of the consistency of percentages of student
   types requesting a given course.
2. Double checking, the means to check the consistency of
   percentage of total requests for the various student
   types.
3. Identification of potential time conflicts arising from
   scheduling at the same time courses which are normally
   taken by the same student types.
4. Comparison of the results of the heuristic approach with
   the regression approach.

Furthermore, with changes in curriculum, it is believed that
there will be an improvement in the ability to forecast the
changes in the percentages of course requests by various student
types. A change in curriculum really shifts the goal posts of
forecasting in that a change in the requirement structure will
most certainly change the way in which students request courses.
When this happens, regression equations will be worth very
little, but the heuristic procedure can still be functional by
estimating new percentages through statistical sampling.

Departmental sector. The simulation of the departmental
sector employs a "decision-rule" or logical approach rather
than the more scientific econometric approach used in the
student sector. It would be impractical to attempt to forecast
the schedule of course offerings on the basis of historical
data. Not only would it be an extremely complex task, but the
variable time mix of the course schedules, variable instructor
assignments, and so on, would make historical data a highly
unreliable basis for a predictive tool.

Each department has the responsibility of determining the
following six decision variables:

1. The courses to be offered.
2. The number of sections of each course.
3. Enrollment limits.
4. Meeting times.
5. Meeting places.
6. Instructor assignments.

Since there are twenty-nine separate departments making decisions in each of the above areas, there are twenty-nine sets of decision rules to be simulated by the model.

The objective for this sector of the model is to effectively and logically describe each department's method of performing its scheduling function.

A number of factors influence the decision variables of the departmental sector. Among these factors are the following:

1. Faculty teaching time preferences.
2. Faculty course preferences.
3. Faculty availability.
4. Faculty priorities.
5. Course priorities.
6. Previous year's student course requests.

Additionally, each department has several departmental policy variables:

1. Teaching loads.
2. Desired course capacities (or student service levels).
3. Enrollment limits.
4. Timing of instructor assignments; e.g., an instructor may teach all his courses on the same day.
5. Number of preparations.

The logic of the simulation of a particular department will depend to a great extent on the policies of that department with regard to preferences, priorities, and general procedures. In order to develop a point of departure for the departmental simulations a model was developed of an hypothetical department. Efforts have been made to revise and fine-tune this model to describe the activity of each of the twenty nine departments.

This particular hypothetical model is based on the following assumptions about departmental policies.

1. Each instructor presents to the department's schedule a list of preferences for courses and teaching times.

2. The department schedule resolves course and time conflicts on the basis of instructor priorities.

3. Courses which are taught by only one instructor are assigned before other course assignments are made.

4. Any course which can be taught by more than one instructor is assigned to the instructor with the highest preference level. In the case of two instructors having the same preference level, instructor priority determines assignment.

5. For each section of each course the meeting time and meeting place are assigned to the priority and time preference of the instructor assigned to that course. There can be as many sections meeting at the same time period as there are rooms assigned to the departments.

A partial description of the variables in the model is provided in Table 10. The logic of the model is displayed in Figure 10. Figure 11 is a sample of the output (departmental course offerings).

Although the individual departmental models are being produced for use in the simulation model, it will be possible to suggest schedules which will be more realistic in satisfying student demand and in space utilization.

Potentialities, degree of completion, and problems. Figure 9 describes, in general, the way in which the three sectors of the model are interrelated, and the appendix sets forth the logic of the general model. In the departmental sector, course offerings are determined as described in Table 10. The course offerings of the individuals departments are combined to produce the master schedule which is presented to the student sector for determination of demand. From the simulated demand a new master schedule could be produced on the basis of forecast demand from the previous simulation run. Moreover, space may be reallocated when it is seen that the old space allocation leads to inefficient use of facilities. Policy changes in

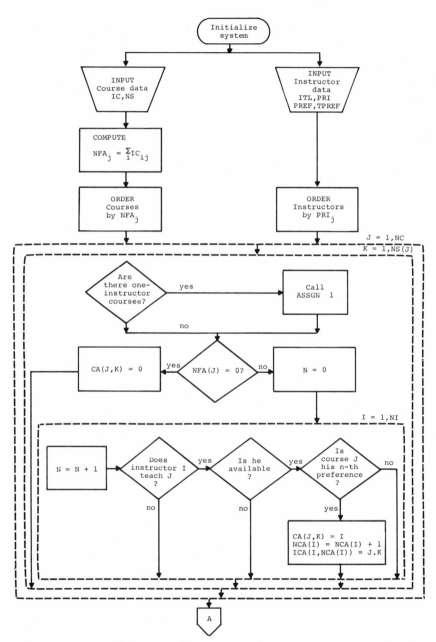

Figure 10. *A model of a departmental sector*

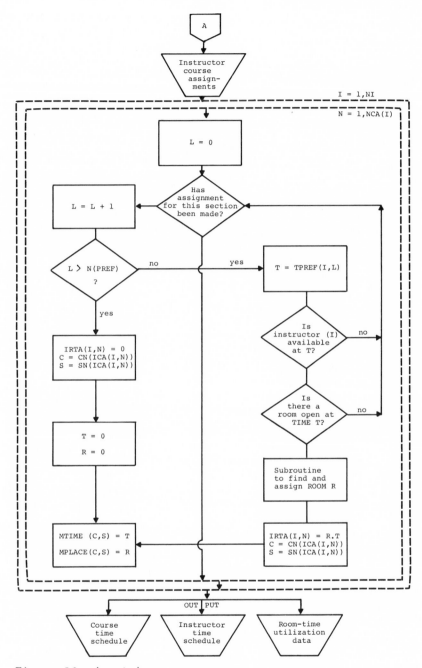

Figure 10. *(cont.)*

Table 10. *Departmental sector variables*

Exogenous variables

$*IC_{ij}$ Instructor course matrix. If the i-th instructor is available to teach the j-th course. $IC_{ij} = 1$; otherwise $IC_{ij} = 0$.

$*NFA_j$ Number of faculty available to teach the j-th course: $NFA_j = \sum_i IC_{ij}$.

NS_j Number of sections to be offered of the j-th course.

NO_j Numerical order of j-th course. Courses are ordered for instructor assignment on the basis of NFA_j; e.g., for the course with the least (nonzero) number of instructors available, an attempt will be made to assign an instructor to it first.

ITL_i The teaching load of the i-th instructor.

PRI_i The priority of the i-th instructor.

$PREF_{in}$ The n-th course preference of the i-th instructor.

$TPREF_{in}$ The n-th time preference of the i-th instructor.

Status variables

NI   Number of instructors.
NC   Number of courses.
NR   Number of rooms.
NTP   Number of time periods.

Endogenous variables

NCA_i Number of courses assigned to the i-th instructor.

ICA_{in} The n-th assignment made to the i-th instructor. The value stored is the index number of the assigned course and section: e.g.,

> Course number   = CN
> Section number = SN
> ICA_{in} = CN + SN/100

CA_{jk} The index number of the instructor assigned to the k-th section of the j-th course.

$IRTA_{in}$ Instructor room-time assignments. For the n-th course assignment of the i-th instructor the index numbers of the room and time assignments are stored: e.g.,

> Room number   = RN
> Time period number = TN
> $IRTA_{in}$ = RN + TN/100

$MTIME_{jk}$ The meeting time of the k-th section of the j-th course.

$MPLACE_{jk}$ The meeting place of the k-th section of the j-th course.

$RMHR_{rt}$ The course assigned for the t-th time period in the r-th room.

*These variables are changed by the system but are initially exogenous.

scheduling, as well as curriculum will effect changes in classroom utilization, instructor utilization, student and faculty
satisfaction, and a host of other response variables. The
effects of these changes can be examined with this model.

DEPARTMENT OF BULL

COURSE	SECTION	MEETING TIME	MEETING PLACE	INSTRUCTOR
1	1	MWF 4	MADDOX HALL 229	ALLEN, I. VAN
1	2	MWF 2	BRYAN HALL 104	ALLEN, I. VAN
1	3	MWF 5	SOC. SCI. 305	FARQUARD, J.P.
1	4	TBA	TBA	TBA
63	1	MWF 3	SOC. SCI. 305	LING, DING A.
63	2	MWF 4	SOC. SCI. 305	LING, DING A.
63	3	MWF 5	BRYAN HALL 104	LING, DING A.
101	1	MWF 1	BRYAN HALL 104	FARQUARD, J.P.
101	2	MWF 3	MADDOX HALL 229	FARQUARD, J.P.
132	1	MWF 4	BRYAN HALL 104	REDDY, R.U.
132	2	TBA	TBA	TBA
132	3	TBA	TBA	TBA
220	1	MWF 3	BRYAN HALL 104	REDDY, R.U.

Figure 11. *Sample departmental output*

At the date of this writing the aggregate model is near
completion; the forecasting model (student sector) is in the
validation stage, while the departmental sector is being fine-
tuned for application. Data are being collected through inter-
views for use in the departmental sector model. An attempt is
now being made to coordinate the three sectors of the model into
one working model, and policies are being adapted to logical
description for test-run purposes.

The major problems which have been incurred in the development of this model are data-related. For the departmental model,

the type of data needed to provide adequate description of the
decision rules used is difficult to obtain for several reasons.
Here are two:

1. Departments are reluctant to divulge information because
of a general fear of "computers" and loss of control.

2. Many of the decision rules and procedures and much of the
data used by the departments are not well-defined or may exist
only in the minds of the schedulers.

For the student sector, model problems have been incurred in
acquiring an adequate data base for forecasting. There is a
general dearth of data in this area in machine-retrievable form.
In some cases the data that did exist had to be cross-filed in
order to be useful.

Appendix - *The general model*

The following is a conception of the logic of the general
model of the entire system (see Figure 9.)

I. Inputs

   A. Space inventory

      1. Rooms are classified by room type.
         (a) General type (laboratories, lecture rooms, re-
            citation).
         (b) Special teaching facilities (maps, visual aids,
            etc.).
      2. Data on location, numbers of seats, etc.

   B. Time structure

      The master time schedule dictating at what hours classes
      may begin and end is considered an input. The time
      structure is normally fixed, but could be considered a
      potential administrative change variable and hence is
      included for policy simulation purposes.

   C. Faculty availability

      For any given period, the faculty available to teach
      is assumed to be fixed and known. However, this vari-
      able as an input is subject to change. For a given
      course, faculty availability is a function of:

(1) the number of instructors who are capable of teaching that course, (2) the teaching loads of these faculty members, and (3) the number of sections of other courses assigned to these faculty members.

D. Student background data

1. Number of students enrolled.
2. Number of students in each major.

II. On the basis of some decision-rule (e.g., one room to every eleven sections offered the previous semester) the administrative sector assigns rooms to the departments for primary use by that department.

III. A simulation model will be constructed to describe each department's activities in determining the course schedule.

Chapter ten. The use of a scheduling algorithm in a gaming environment for administrative planning.

Ronald L. Jensen, Martin L. Levin, William W. Pendleton, and Norman P. Uhl

Increasingly, colleges and universities are faced with difficult decisions regarding the assignment of existing classroom and office space and the allocation of funds for expanding such facilities. Curricular innovation, the expansion of facilities, increased enrollment, expanding research programs, and student activities combine to pose major and often conflicting demands for the reallocation of existing facilities and for special consideration in assigning priorities in plans for expansion. There is every reason to believe that these competing demands will grow rather than abate during the coming decades. Only the wealthiest schools will be able to provide sufficient space for all demands while employing traditional patterns of space utilization. Even for them, the basic problems may remain, since the demand for space in universities seems always to exceed what is available by a constant factor.

The research described in this paper is being conducted at Emory University. Private schools such as Emory have special problems — or perhaps share problems to a special degree. Though better able than some state schools to limit enrollment, their building programs are difficult to finance. Thus, even in the long run a dramatic expansion program is unlikely; and for the short term, in which most of us must live, more efficient utilization of existing resources seems the only acceptable course.

The basic question of what utilization pattern is efficient for a university is not easily answered. Those who compete for the resources of the university have divergent views. Two faculty members in an office may decrease the need for offices but also decrease the effectiveness, if not the quality, of the faculty. Classes at 7:00 a.m. may increase the utilization of classrooms but adversely affect the process of learning. Yet, short of the Elysian prospect of huge construction grants, extreme suggestions such as these seem to be all that is available to the decision maker.

Emory confronted this dilemma, and finding such alternatives unacceptable, took up the questions of utilization in the following way: Can more space be allocated to faculty and research without penalizing the students in choice of courses and number of class periods per day? If such penalties exist, what is their magnitude in terms of course conflicts and number of class periods? What schedule and space allocations will be acceptable to the university? Although our approach to the problem is in some ways specific to our situation and our efforts are toward an acceptable rather than a theoretically optimal solution, it is hoped that the groundwork can be laid for similar efforts in other university settings.

Traditional approaches

An approach to solving space utilization problems is the application of computer-based models of course scheduling. Early attempts to use a computer as an aid in scheduling were primarily transfers of paper-and-pencil techniques to the computer. These procedures assumed that a master schedule had been prepared and assigned students to the schedule according to various rules which would minimize conflicts (by trying to assign all students to the courses they had requested), restrict class enrollments to specified upper limits, and perhaps meet one or two other minor requirements. This approach had the primary limitations of restricting the student's freedom in selecting courses and requiring the same advanced manual preparation of a master schedule as did paper-and-pencil techniques. Freedom in selecting courses may not be especially important in some institutional settings, but it is highly desirable in scheduling most college and university programs. The greater the flexibility in course selection permitted by a college, the less likely it is that a master schedule will satisfy the needs of the students. A common scheduling system used by many larger universities assigns students to multisectioned courses, where the sections are offered at different

times during the day, to increase the likelihood that each
student desiring the course will be able to find a section
which fits his schedule. This system is of limited value to
the smaller university or college where each course may be a
single section or where there are very few sectioned courses.

Because these early scheduling procedures required a master
schedule, the utility of their results was very much dependent
upon the quality of the initial master schedule. Unfortunately,
there are few criteria by which the quality of a master schedule
can be determined beforehand. To explore by hand the useful-
ness of different master schedules is inefficient because of
the effort required to prepare several feasible master schedules.

The problem of developing a master schedule was recognized
fairly early in the development of scheduling approaches, but
has proved elusive. The creation of a feasible and desirable
master schedule has been complicated by the tremendous number
of variables involved and the complexity of their relationships.
In developing such master schedules, the goal has often been
an "optimal" schedule. Since not all colleges and universities
have the same objectives, constraints, resources, or policies,
the term "optimal" has meaning only when defined in the context
of those factors. For that reason it has not been possible to
develop programs which are optimal in an inherent sense. Rather,
programs have been sought that will achieve a specific set of
goals in specific situations.

One general way to provide an "optimal"solution for a wide
range of conditions is to apply the linear programing concept
to scheduling. This approach to the allocation of resources
has been successful in a variety of settings, and the algorithm
is quite general in its presentation. Harding demonstrated in
a study[1] that a linear-programing formulation of the scheduling
problem which will recognize almost any number of constraints
and objectives is theoretically possible; but he indicated that,
for a scheduling problem of any size, the number of variables
and constraints rapidly surpasses the capacity of any existing
computer or algorithm. Moreover, the set-up cost of this
approach is quite high, especially where conditions change
rapidly. Thus, given the present state of the art, linear
programing is unwieldy even for relatively small problems.

Another approach suggested by Holzman and Turkes[2] utilizes Boolean algebra in examining the scheduling problem and determining the set of feasible solutions which contain zero conflicts for student and faculty schedules. They demonstrate that this set may be quite large and that the zero conflict condition may easily demand a schedule with more class periods than are possible. This approach has been used more frequently in studying the problems of scheduling than in establishing an operational scheduling system. However, it does provide additional insight into the scheduling problem.

A number of scheduling systems have been proposed and placed in operation with the objective of creating master schedules. These systems have been designed primarily for high-school scheduling and frequently involve assumptions or restrictions which are unacceptable in many university settings. For example, it is not uncommon to assign teachers to courses first and then produce a time schedule which has zero conflicts for the teachers. This time schedule is then treated as the master schedule and student assignments made accordingly. The first stage of this approach is inappropriate for most colleges and universities because the assignment of teachers to courses has been the prerogative of the academic dean or the department head, who must balance many factors other than scheduling as he assigns instructors to courses. These approaches are also characterized by restrictions on the students' freedom to choose courses.

A proposed model

In the project being reported here, the approach to the development of a scheduling model tries to overcome the restrictions on the students' freedom to choose courses by searching for satsifactory rather than optimal solutions. This approach begins with a curriculum as well as the course selections of the students and employs the model to develop a master schedule which considers students, faculty, and available space.[3] Through its integration into a gaming environment, the model may prove useful in evaluating certain decisions about prospective resource allocation. A description of the model follows, and one procedure for accomplishing such an integration.

For many schools like Emory, the assignment of faculty to courses is largely dependent upon the instructor's competence in and preference for certain courses. Even the few sectioned courses are taught by a small, determinable faculty group; therefore, it is possible to indicate the instructors for all courses and sections. Each course-instructor combination is unique, and the students may select their courses and sections as if each were a single-section selection. Moreover, a primary assumption of this model is that the student should have maximum opportunity to obtain his preferred course selections, i.e., course conflicts should be minimized. When course conflicts do exist, some are recognized as being more restrictive than others — e.g., conflicts for a senior are more restrictive than are those for a freshman. Therefore, weights are assigned to conflicts which force the model to adjust the schedule according to assumed scales of conflict disutility.

Assigning instructors to courses is exogenous to the model, since, as indicated above, the assignment of instructors is the prerogative of the academic dean of department head at Emory. Moreover, instructor assignment is inappropriate for a scheduling model if the student is to be allowed to consider the instructor in choosing courses. It is impossible to allow students to select from a list of courses with assigned instructors, and then allow the scheduling model to use their selections in turn to assign the instructors. It is a simple matter to extend the concept of weighting conflicts so that the assignment of two or more classes, taught by the same instructor, to the same hour will not occur.

In its initial form, the model does not attempt to handle such problems as the prima donna instructor who does not want to teach before 10:00 a.m. These problems are left to manual methods, if they are to be considered at all. However, because of the extreme modular construction of the model, it is possible to add refinements to incorporate such considerations. The immediate price for such refinements is a larger program, which could require a larger computer for execution or additional running time, with the accompanying expense. Moreover, such additional constraints increase the probability of unresolved conflicts in other areas by reducing the degree of freedom in the model.

The model also assumes a simple course assignment schedule with n identical days during the week and seeks courses of uniform time length t. It is a relatively simple modification to allow unequal time lengths as long as all classes are scheduled for an integral number of subunits, such as half-hour increments. The model modifications necessary to handle nonidentical days are more extensive. These have not been considered here, because Emory treats instructional weekdays as equivalent for scheduling purposes.

The model is constructed to assign classes to preferred locations (such as specific instructional buildings), but if a preferred location is not available, it uses whatever space can be found. At this time, the problem of specifying any schedule for secondary preferences does not appear to justify the added expense of complexity and size of the program.

The model schedules classes in the following manner.

1. A matrix of weighted conflicts, with weights selected according to the importance of the conflicts, is established.

2. On the assumption that large classes with many conflicts are the most difficult to handle, the largest course, from the set of courses with the maximum weighted number of conflicts, is assigned first.

3. The course (in the set of courses not conflicting with the one assigned) with the largest number of other conflicts is selected and assigned to the same time period.

4. Step 3 is repeated for additional courses as long as there are classrooms available in the prime location areas.

5. When courses or rooms available for assignment are exhausted, the next time slot is used.

6. The process is repeated until all time slots are used.

7. To schedule any remaining classes, the entire procedure is repeated after removing the restriction of assigning classes to the preferred location. At the end of this phase the model will have reached the situation where all available rooms have been assigned or all zero conflict assignments have been made.

8. Assuming space is not exhausted, the only classes remaining to be assigned are those which produce conflicts of some sort. The model now becomes suboptimal in that it moves into a routine which simply takes each remaining course and

assigns it to a time slot where it produces a minimum number
of conflicts with the courses already assigned. (This portion
of the algorithm is being studied in the hope of improving it,
and the final version may be quite different from that described.)

9. At the completion of the assignment section, the model
prepares a report on:

(a) The course time schedule with the number of conflicts
    for each hour.
(b) The schedule of room assignments and a listing of
    rooms not used.
(c) A listing of any courses which could not be assigned
    due to lack of space.
(d) A listing of the students with conflicts.

The responsible administrator thus has all of the necessary
information with which to seek an extraordinary solution for
the remaining conflicts.

Computerized scheduling models in a gaming environment

Computerized scheduling models appear to offer an opportunity
for a broad approach to examining projected resource demand
schedules. If such models enable the *administrator* to utilize
more efficiently available resources (given actual demand schedules and actual resources), they can also allow the *decision
maker* to examine the impact of projected demand schedules on
hypothetical resource configurations.[4] What is proposed here
is to use the scheduling model in a gaming environment, i.e.,
to allow the decision maker to manipulate both the inputs
(demand schedule) and constraints (resources available) in the
scheduling model and observe the consequences of the manipulations for the output (the schedules) from the model.

In this system the decision maker plays a series of games
with the scheduling model, analyzing the feasibility of the
outcomes and comparing the relative advantage of each game.
The output of an episode with the scheduling model which will
be of interest to the decision maker is the conflict matrix.

This contains the record of students who requested courses
which were scheduled at the same hour. It also contains either
a record of the courses which could not be scheduled because
space was not available or a record of the space which was not
utilized. Thus, by playing the game, the decision maker is in
a position to compare the conflict matrices from a series of
episodes in which he had varied the inputs or constraints, or
both, and assess the utility of such variations.

Not all possible manipulations of inputs and constraints
are meaningful. The decision maker must choose those manipulations which can be translated into policy decisions in order
for the gaming outcome to have practical application. Within
the context of Emory's situation a number of such manipulations
are discussed below.

It is assumed that the criteria for a "reasonable schedule"
are known to the decision maker. Most likely these criteria
involve some number of course conflicts among the students and
some number of courses which could not be scheduled due to lack
of classroom space. The decision rules which go to make up the
criteria will, in general, be the prerogative of the decision
maker.

The model produces a schedule within the context of a set
of constraints or inputs. The major constraints of interest
here are:

(a) The courses to be offered.
(b) The classrooms.
(c) The capacity of the classrooms.
(d) The number of class periods in the instructional day.
(e) The course selections of the students.

Any of the five constraints may be manipulated for purposes
of the game, and the reports of the model may be analyzed to
determine the consequences of such manipulations. Although
more than one constraint can be manipulated at the same time,
the nature of the questions the decision maker may pose can
best be illustrated by examining each separately.

The courses offered.   If a significant number of courses are
added to the curriculum, two important questions are raised.

(1) What will be the impact on the demand for resources?   (2) Can a reasonable schedule be devised? Except under the most unusual conditions these questions are not easily answered by inspection. It is not a simple matter of looking to see if there are classrooms with enough capacity in which to schedule the new courses. However, if the answer to such a question is yes, the problem does disappear. The other side of the coin is the more interesting situation, for the introduction of new courses may reduce the enrollments in other courses and hence allow them to be scheduled in smaller classrooms. The game should provide the deicision maker with much more reliable data on the consequences of this new policy.

It should be mentioned that the question the decision maker is posing here is one of great moment, given the current turmoil in institutions of higher education. In response to student interest, new programs are proliferating at an unprecedented rate, and too often the planning for these programs is haphazard or nonexistent.

The classrooms and the capacity of classrooms. At Emory, and likely at other institutions, the need has increased not only for instructional space but also for research space, faculty offices, and auxiliary instructional space, such as statistical laboratories and lounge areas where students and faculty can meet informally. Since the needs are immediate, the solution often has been to partition a classroom into a smaller classroom and an office or to devote the entire classroom to purposes other than teaching formal courses. Although there have been forecasts of impending doom whenever this procedure has been employed, somehow things have generally worked out. This is probably due in part to the fact that classroom space at Emory has been underutilized. Classes of fifteen have been meeting in rooms designed to hold fifty students, and classrooms have gone unassigned for several periods of the instructional day. However, there is a limit to this solution, and the decision as to which classroom is to be sacrificed should be made on rational grounds.

Using the procedure proposed here, the decision maker can play a game with the classroom and classroom capacity constraints. For example, if one classroom with a capacity of

fifty students is altered to make a student-faculty lounge and
another of the same capacity is altered to make two classrooms
with a capacity of twenty students each, what will be the impact on the schedule? Certainly, the results of such a game
would be better than educated guesses.

   The number of class periods in the instructional day. This
constraint operates rather peculiarly at Emory. For many years,
most of the undergraduate courses have been scheduled in a
three-hour instructional day starting at nine in the morning.
Recently, there has been a slight increase in the number of
courses meeting at noon, 8:00 a.m., and other hours.[5] Both
faculty and students have come to view the meeting of courses
during the prime hours as a right rather than a privilege.
Yet, all concerned recognize that the day may come when this
situation must change. But how drastic must the change be?
Need we go to an eight-hour instructional day, or will a five-
hour day suffice? The problem is more complex than merely
expanding the number of hours for the assignment of these
undergraduate courses. The undergraduate college at Emory
includes slightly less than half the total full-time student
body, and it shares both classroom space and faculty with the
graduate school and several of the professional schools. Consequently, changes in policy for the undergraduate program can
create the need for changes in policy within the other divi-
sions. Such changes may or may not be desirable, and the game
can provide information to help in choosing between alternatives.

   The course selections of the students. While the course
selections of the students cannot be directly manipulated in a
meaningful way, the conditions which produce the resultant
configuration can. For example, a change in curricular requirements will produce a change in the courses selected and in the
timing of the selection of the courses. Once it is determined
how a curricular change will affect course selections, the new
selections can be used in the game and the impact of the curricular change on the schedule observed. Of course, the determination of the manner in which these changes affect course
selection is exogenous to the game.

One approach to determining the impact of such modifications is being tried at Emory. A Monte Carlo simulation of student course selection is being developed based upon various characteristics of the students and estimates of the probability of students selecting certain courses at certain points in their career. To illustrate, a male chemistry major from a rural high school may have a different probability of taking a mythology course as a sophomore than a female history major from an urban high school in her sophomore year. Those probabilities are calculated from data gathered on the past course selections of students with the characteristics in question. Moreover, an analysis is under way to determine which, if any, demographic and social characteristics of students have important effects upon their course selections. The output of this simulation is a set of course selections which is analogous to a set of actual selections.

Among the inputs to the Monte Carlo simulation are (1) the distribution of students by categories, each category representing a characteristic related to course selection, (2) the course selection probabilities associated with each category, and (3) the total number of students in the simulated population. Any or all of these parameters may be manipulated independently in generating a simulated set of course selections.

By using the simulation output as input to the game, the decision maker can manipulate the simulation inputs as part of the game and thus increase the scope of his questions. He can then pose questions of the following order:

What will be the impact upon the schedule of admitting a higher proportion of females than called for by current policy?

If an additional hundred students is admitted, what demands on classroom space can be expected?

Moreover, if some courses are assigned an upper limit on section enrollment size (and the decision maker has knowledge of existing faculty resources), it would be possible for him to estimate the need for additional faculty to support increases in the number of students and changes in the demographic mix of the student body. Projections could also be made as to which academic departments would experience the most pressing needs for additional faculty.

Summary

This paper has suggested two potentially fruitful paths toward solving problems of short-run resource allocation in institutions of higher education. First, a satisfactory rather than an optimal scheduling model, and second, the use of this model in a gaming environment. It is worth noting that the integration of a scheduling model in the gaming environment does not *require* the scheduling model described herein. There are no obvious reasons why other scheduling models cannot be similarly integrated and used to generate prospective data on resource demands. Indeed, it would seem advantageous for the decision maker to play the same game (holding inputs constant) using a series of scheduling models each based on different assumptions and with different goals. Policy decisions based on such procedures should prove very effective.

Notes

1. Robert E. Harding, "The Linear Programming Approach to Master Time Schedule Generation in Education," in *Optimal Scheduling in Educational Institutions*, ed. A. G. Holzman and W. R. Turkes, Cooperative Research Project No. 1323, University of Pittsburgh, 1964.
2. Holzman and Turkes.
3. The curriculum is taken as given for the model's purposes. At Emory the curriculum for a given quarter is prepared by each department and coordinated by the academic dean.
4. The decision maker and the administrator may be the same individual. The former term is used when considering policy-planning activities.
5. This does not mean that these classrooms sit idle for the remainder of the instructional day. Graduate courses and special seminars for undergraduates are assigned to these rooms after the basic undergraduate courses have been scheduled.